"Look at what we can become . . . "

Look at What
We Can
Become

Portraits of Five
Michaelic Individuals

†

Neill Reilly

SteinerBooks | 2019

SteinerBooks
An imprint of Anthroposophic Press, Inc.
402 Union St. No. 58, Hudson, NY 12534
www.steinerbooks.org

Some quoted translations have been revised.

Design: William Jens Jensen
Cover image: Saint Michael statue
outside San Sebastiano Church,
Panicale, Italy (photo by the author)

Library of Congress Control Number: 2019902985

ISBN: 978-1-62148-246-8 (paperback)
ISBN: 978-1-62148-247-5 (ebook)

Contents

THANKS TO

Andy Leaf
J. Bruce Murphy
Paul O'Leary
Elizabeth Lombardi
Andy Ward
Jennifer Greene
Gene Gollogly
Jens Jensen
&
Debbie Shriver
for their editing and support

"Seek and ye shall find."

Matthew 7:7

Foreword

J. Bruce Murphy

Have you not stopped in a field,
Struck suddenly by the beauty of one particular flower,
Be it alone or among others?
It spoke directly to you;
It gave you joy, gladness, comfort.
So may one be to others like that flower.

CLAIRE BLATCHFORD, *Turning*

The following really happened. In the early 1990s at a Waldorf school conference, I overheard two people speaking about a bell collection that one of them had seen at the school where he worked. He described a large collection of bells that someone traveled around with to display to schoolchildren and to other groups. It was the most impressive collection of bells he had ever seen.

When the owner of the collection made his presentation, he would describe the many different bells and how they were intended to be used. There were large bells and small bells, fine gold and silver bells, ancient bells and more modern bells, coarse and crude bells made of wood and leather, bells for warning and bells for celebration, bells that were musical, and sacred bells that were for use in religious ceremonies. It took nearly an hour to describe all the bells that were in his extensive collection.

The person to whom this was being told asked if the owner of the collection ever rang the bells. "No," said the one telling the story, "as a matter of fact, he never rang any of the bells!"

Wow! That says it all. We talk a lot of abstractions about life, but do we really live?

The people described in this collection of short essays really did ring the bell. The notes that they struck rang true and continue to sound and resound effectively in the world.

There is plenty of "dry-land swimming," but few of us actually want to get wet. We are happier discussing swimming techniques or standing on the shore to watch others swim. "Today when people speak of the spirit, most people mean something abstract and unfitted for the world, and not something that can make an impact on everyday life" (Rudolf Steiner, *Ideas for a New Europe,* p. 3).

There are five individuals pictured in these sketches. And oh, they were individuals! Each is one of a kind. There is a scholar, a leader, a teacher, an activist, and an actor. Of course, each is more than just one word can describe.

Professor Fritz Koelln, the scholar, was a teacher of the highest grade. John Gardner, the leader, was also a teacher, as was Lee Lecraw who defined "Ladyhood" (can that even be said in these "pronoun-conscious" times?). Marjorie Spock, also a teacher, was an activist (an activist who actually got things done), and actor/playwright William Ward was a most accomplished and courageous Waldorf class teacher.

It almost goes without saying that to describe these often controversial persons may just invite more controversy. Some might wish for more about the subjects under consideration, but that is beside the point, which is that those portrayed give us something to look up to and encourage us for life.

The descriptions of the subjects depicted here are excellent. The picture of Fritz Koelln with his vitality, piercing blue eyes, zest for life, enthusiasm, and practicality is spot on. The description of John Gardner as being eminently cordial, quintessentially American, self-disciplined, and grounded gets to the nub of who John was. Lee Lecraw is lovingly described. She was the picture of grit, grace, and strength striving to "make it real." Marjorie Spock's lifelong quest was born of "fearless knowledge and a really strong will" and was utterly practical. William Ward's dramatic style, storytelling ability, and "puckish sense of humor" are in evidence in this sketch portraying his "journey into the light."

They are each "Souls who choose love over hate, love over greed, love over power, Souls who chose in this life to do My will, who were born with Yes in the deepest part of their souls" (Reilly, *Songs and Dreams*, p. 49). Though each was an individual, they shared certain characteristics. They were all teachers. Each one acknowledged a connection to Anthroposophy and Rudolf Steiner and each has passed on to the next world (which of course is part of this world in which we live). Each demonstrated an understanding that human beings must transform themselves before they can undertake their tasks in the right way.

The lives of the individuals sketched here also share the need to be free. These portraits describe individuals who strive to realize freedom in a manner suited to each individual.

Rudolf Steiner dedicated his seminal work, *The Philosophy of Freedom,* to such people:

> …things we do not fully comprehend are repugnant to the individual element in us, which wants to experience every-thing in the depths of its inner being. The only knowledge

that satisfies us is one that is subject to no external standards but springs from the inner life of the personality....

Each of us claims the right to start from the facts that lie nearest to hand, from our own immediate experiences, and thence to ascend to knowledge of the whole universe. We strive for certainty in knowledge, but each in our own way....

I am under no illusion about the characteristics of my time. I know how much the tendency prevails to make things impersonal and stereotyped. But I also know equally well that many of my contemporaries try to order their lives in the kind of way I have indicated. *To them I would dedicate this book.*" (Steiner, *The Philosophy of Freedom,* author's prefaces, p. xxviii, emphasis added)

Each of the five people described here lived in the way that each felt best fulfilled the desire to be free. Sometimes they were in perfect harmony with their surroundings, and at other times they lived in active opposition to their times. But they always lived in a way that let the spirit shine through. "[We] must realize how the world would be transformed if the meaning of freedom were understood, freedom not in the sense of license, but freedom born of a free spirit and a firmly disciplined mind" (Steiner, *From Symptom to Reality in Modern History,* p. 156).

The importance of the pictures painted here of these individuals lies not so much in singing the praises of great women and men as in the uplift that these examples grant to our souls. These lives, well lived, evoke in us feelings of admiration and respect. Respect and admiration, not so much for the persons described, but of the possibilities that are part of a human being's intrinsic nature.

Development occurs within the individual. None were static. In each case the second act (or in some cases the third act) was far better than the first. All show real growth. Development in an individual is not just a phrase or abstraction. It is in evidence. It inspires us. Who can help but feel raised up by such possibilities? As Rudolf Steiner stated, we must embrace becoming: "It is still always possible as a person to become something.... People strive to delude themselves in regard to this necessity of becoming something. Most of all, they endeavor to call attention to what they are, not to what they will become" (Steiner, *The Challenge of the Times*, p. 127).

Also, there is the acknowledgment that things happen only when some person makes them happen There may be ideas whose time has come, but it is up to the individual to bring these ideas to life and incorporate them into the world and bring them to fruition. The five souls described here lived their lives in such a way.

Depicted for us here are heroes of the spirit who "struggle to free oneself from the superficial impression of the senses, and to find the spirit within the world of the senses" (Steiner, *Christianity as Mystical Fact*, p. 29).

Look at What We Can Become is a call to each of us to harken unto to what lies deepest in our souls with courage, the ever present help of the spiritual world and good humor.

You cannot help but love the individuals so lovingly brought before us here. It is also good for us to hear their stories, whether or not we have personal knowledge of the people celebrated here. They bring us "joy, gladness, comfort."

NB: In the section concerning Fritz Koelln, "Fritz's boys" at Bowdoin College is mentioned. In the interest of full disclosure, I am everlastingly grateful to be fortunate enough to be one of "Fritz's boys."

Introduction

As a child, I was fortunate to have been in the presence of my elderly, Irish grandmothers. My parents dedicated themselves to their children and their parents. My parents could not abide the idea of a nursing home for their parents. We crammed nine people into a small four-bedroom house. There were two people in a room and three boys in one room. Sometimes my Nanny O'Neill also slept in the boys' room. She and I shared a bed at times.

My grandmothers were extremely kind, generous souls who had lovely, lilting brogues. Their speech had "a touch of the poet" in it. To this day I think of old age and brogues as gifts to anyone who encounters them. Since I was the youngest, I was called the *gossoon*, which is Irish for a young boy. My grandmothers were my protection from the taunts of my older brothers. I could run to my nannies' bedrooms for sanctuary. These loving relationships and the respect of my parents for my grandmothers were the source of my affection for older people. Since my experience with them had been so heart warming, I inherently trusted older people. My young soul gravitated to older souls. This blossomed into my friendships with many people dramatically older than I was. I met Professor Fritz Koelln when I was twenty-one, and he was sixty-nine. He was forty-eight years older than I was.

Years later, in my thirties, I would often take my wife and children to visit older friends in New England. Once we visited a couple who were close to my age. My nine-year-old daughter looked troubled and confused upon meeting them. She had an intuitive understanding of non-trustworthy individuals. She asked me to speak with her. She said, "Are you sure these people are your friends?" I thought to myself, "Had I misread my friends? Was there something amiss with them?" I stated "Yes, they are my friends, why are you so concerned?" She exclaimed her confusion "But they are so young!"

Like my grandmothers, these five individuals resonated in my heart and soul. These portraits are of beloved individuals, older friends who have crossed over to the other side. They were all teachers connected with Anthroposophy and Waldorf schools. Each one was a unique individual who gladly offered her talents to educate students.

I knew Professor Koelln for more than fifteen years and knew John Gardner and Lee Lecraw for decades. I knew Marjorie Spock and William Ward for only a few years and had far fewer interactions with them, so I can share fewer intimate stories about them. This does not mean that they are less remarkable than the others. I just have fewer stories to tell. Therefore their portraits are shorter, with more quotations from relevant books.

These are portraits, not biographies. These are short sketches. They are not objective in the usual sense of the word. However the subjectivity is merited because I love these individuals. I have written about them precisely because I love them, flaws and all. The portraits are fond remembrances of departed souls. That does not mean these subjective and deeply personal portraits are not valid for others. Each reader can test and determine the validity of the portraits. In that sense they are objectively verifiable. If the critique is that the author is too fond of his subjects, I plead guilty as charged.

One might wonder why there are so many quotations by Dr. Rudolf Steiner in these portraits. Are these portraits of these individuals or an exegesis on Dr. Rudolf Steiner? The answer is both. The reason for the centrality of Steiner's ideas and ideals is because they motivated these individuals throughout their lives. Each of them took Steiner's works very seriously. Their lives and actions demonstrated the realization of that understanding. Imagine a Shakespearean scholar who does not incorporate the wisdom of Shakespeare into daily life. Or better yet, a Christian who does not live according to a genuine relationship with the Bible. These brave souls decided to lead countercultural lives. They were not fascinated with the modern attachments to money, fame, and power. They were seekers in the purest sense of the word. They had come to Earth to find their mission.

Rudolf Steiner stated that in 1879 the Archangel Michael became the Spirit of the Age. Michael, like John the Baptist, is a forerunner to Christ. He prepares His way. In 1884 or 1886, Pope Leo XII had a horrific vision regarding the future of humanity. He wrote the famous prayer to St. Michael.

> Saint Michael the Archangel,
> defend us in battle,
> be our protection against the wickedness
> and snares of the devil;
> may God rebuke him, we humbly pray;
> and do thou, O Prince of the heavenly host,
> by the power of God, cast into hell
> Satan and all the evil spirits
> who prowl through the world
> seeking the ruin of souls.
> Amen.

The term *Michaelic* refers to the Archangel Michael, who fights satanic forces. He is often seen in armor, resolute in his demeanor. He gives no quarter to evil. He is intimately connected with Christ. Each of these individuals had Michaelic characteristics. The picture on the cover of this book is of a Michael statue in Panicale, Italy. Note how balanced the Archangel is with one foot on the head of Satan and his sword pointing, but not thrusting, at the head of Satan. Such balance and focus is critical to human endeavors, especially those concerning the spiritual life and education.

It can be a daunting vision when we look at what modern people see before their incarnation. Our perspective is World War I, the Depression, Nazism, Communism, World War II, the Holocaust, nuclear proliferation, all the way to 9/11. The triumph of materialism seems inevitable. But brave souls relish spiritual conflicts; they want to carry the light through the darkness. These five individuals were spiritually brave.

The last challenges of life are old age, sickness, and death. Lee Lecraw would often paraphrase Betty Davis' quip: "Getting old is not for sissies!" A number of us were able to interact with them until their later years. They each aged with dignity and matured spiritually. Professor Fritz Koelln stated that wisdom does not come with old age. If so, all older people would be wise. Rather, one had to work continuously on oneself. "Know Thyself" was the ancient Greek imperative inscribed on the portico of the Temple of Apollo in Delphi. Each of these individuals struggled throughout their lives to know the eternal self. The struggle continued up to and through death. Although as imperfect as the rest of us, this profound struggle gave each of them a balanced understanding of the essence of being human. They had listened to Socrates' warning: "The unexamined life is not worth living" (Plato, *The*

Apology). They examined their lives, and in so doing enriched the lives of countless individuals.

Each of these individuals strove to lead a meaningful life and determined the unique definition of *meaningful*. "Seek and ye shall find" is an accurate statement. These individuals sought the truth, and in doing so they attracted other seekers, who found them. This leads to a community of seekers. Each of these individuals was engaged in community. Groups formed around them, notably study groups and festival groups. Individuality leads to fraternity.

By leading spiritual lives, they prepared for a meaningful end of life and for death. Your end of life is a continuation of your daily life. Therefore, they prepared for the end of life on a daily basis. Socrates stated that idea in *The Phaedo*.

> "Is not what we call death a freeing and separation of soul from body?"
>
> "Certainly," he said.
>
> "And the desire to free the soul is found chiefly, or rather only, in the true philosopher. In fact the philosopher's occupation consists precisely in the freeing and separation of soul from body. Isn't that so?"
>
> "Apparently."
>
> "Well, then, as I said at the beginning, if a man has trained himself throughout his life to live in a state as close as possible to death, would it not be ridiculous for him to be distressed when death comes to him?"
>
> "It would, of course."
>
> "Then it is a fact, Simmias, that true philosophers make dying their profession, and that to them of all men death is least alarming. Look at it in this way. If they are thoroughly dissatisfied with the body, and long to have their souls independent of it, when this happens would it not be entirely unreasonable to be frightened and distressed? Would they

not naturally be glad to set out for the place where there is a prospect of attaining the object of their lifelong desire—which is wisdom—and of escaping from an unwelcome association? Surely there are many who have chosen of their own free will to follow dead lovers and wives and sons to the next world, in the hope of seeing and meeting there the persons whom they loved. If this is so, will a true lover of wisdom who has firmly grasped this same conviction—that he will never attain to wisdom worthy of the name elsewhere than in the next world—will he be grieved at dying? Will he not be glad to make that journey? We must suppose so, my dear boy, that is, if he is a real philosopher, because then he will be of the firm belief that he will never find wisdom in all its purity in any other place. If this is so, would it not be quite unreasonable, as I said just now, for such a man to be afraid of death?"

"It would, indeed."

"So if you see anyone distressed at the prospect of dying, said Socrates, it will be proof enough that he is a lover not of wisdom but of the body. As a matter of fact, I suppose he is also a lover of wealth and reputation—one or the other, or both." (Plato, *Phaedo*, lines 67–69)

This does not mean they had easy lives ora painless ends of their days. Some had severe difficulties in their final days. Each strove to maintain consciousness until the end. To paraphrase St. Paul, they fought the good fight; they finished the race; they kept the faith until the end.

The title for this book comes from another great soul, Hans Pusch. That story is in the essay on Professor Fritz Koelln, but bears repeating. Bruce Murphy once attended a lecture by Professor Koelln and sat near Hans Pusch, Fritz's dear old boyhood and anthroposophic friend. Fritz and Hans grew up together in

Hamburg, Germany. Both Hans and Bruce were amazed by Fritz's dramatic lecture. Hans stated that watching Fritz grow over the years reminded him of the old joke about two rabbits walking down Fifth Avenue. The rabbits stopped at Saks Fifth Avenue and admired a mannequin in a store window. The mannequin was wearing a beautiful rabbit coat. One rabbit said to the other, "Look at what we can become!" Hans was amazed by what Fritz had become and was inspired by his friend's spiritual development.

As I have now reached the age of Fritz when I first met him, I am in even more awe of him. In his seventies, Fritz would travel three hours in my small car from Long Island to Pennsylvania. He would engage in spirited conversations to the very end of his life. He and the other four individuals endured.

When you look at each of these lives, you come away with the impression that only that particular individual could have taken on those tasks. They accepted their karma and used their freedom to address their issues. Their discipline, enthusiasm, and dedication to the spiritual life was contagious. The Irish have a phrase often used at a wake or funeral: "Take a good look. You are unlikely to see another like that again."

I gave the Professor Fritz Koelln essay to a friend who did not know Fritz, and he stated, "I had no idea people like this existed. You are a lucky man!" Yes, indeed.

"Look at What We Can Become..."

Portraits of Five Michaelic Individuals

Professor Fritz C. A. Koelln with Professor Alton Herman Gustafson
Bowdoin College, Brunswick, Maine

Fritz Carl August Koelln

"Each day anew."
GOETHE

I was blessed to have had Professor Fritz Koelln as my teacher. He taught a Bowdoin College senior seminar titled "Friedrich Nietzsche: A Problematic Thinker for Our Time," which was the most challenging and rewarding class I have ever taken. Professor Koelln was sixty-nine years old when he taught this course. He spoke seven languages. He was demanding, profound, and had truly heartfelt, inner warmth. His students could barely keep up with his intellectual vitality. He was like a stellar runner who sets the pace. We just tried to stay as close to him as we could. During classes, we respectfully called him Professor Koelln, but he was known affectionately as *Fritz*.

Fritz Koelln was born in Hamburg, Germany, May 23, 1901. He passed away on September 20, 1986 in Brunswick, Maine. His body was waked in a small study in his home. Then there was a Christian Community service in the Bowdoin College Chapel. It is astounding how the world changed in those eighty-five years. Kali Yuga ended in 1899. Kali Yuga was the age when humanity was completely cut off from the spiritual world. That age saw the height of materialism. Everything was reduced to matter. Spiritual realities were for idle dreamers. The materialism of the modern age had reduced thinking to mere concepts. This split in reality fomented spiritual illness in both individuals and societies. But a light stated to dawn. Steiner refers to 1879 as the beginning of the Michaelic age.

> The Michael Age has arrived. Hearts are beginning to have thoughts. Enthusiasm is no longer generated by obscure mysticism, but by inner clarity supported by thoughts. To grasp this is to receive Michael into one's own being. Thoughts that aim at understanding matters of the spirit in our time must spring from hearts devoted to Michael as the fiery cosmic lord of thought. (Steiner, *The Michael Mystery*, pp. 3 and 4)

Michael is the forerunner of the Second Coming of Christ in the etheric, which Steiner stated began around 1933. It was also the time when dark forces became most virulent as oppositional forces to Christ. Hence the rise of Hitler and Nazism, Lenin, Stalin, and Communism.

Fritz grew up in Germany when it was the intellectual and cultural center of the world. It was the Germany of Goethe, Hegel, Fichte, and Schiller. Germany produced an amazing number of Nobel Prize winners. This changed with the advent of World War I. The forces of modernity are in direct conflict with the Michaelic spirit. After the defeat of Germany in World War I and the severe reparations that followed, Germany became chaotic. Chaos led to the fall of the Weimar Republic, rioting in the streets, hyperinflation, depression, and despair. Germany fell victim to Hitler and Goebbels, a wasteland of hate. The former center of Europe was destroyed.

Fritz had studied in Germany with the leading intellectuals of his time, many of whom were anthroposophists or Jewish. Fritz read Steiner voraciously, but disagreed with Steiner's understanding of Kant. Fritz thought Steiner did not fully understand the genius of Kant's philosophy. Fritz's youthful pride and arrogance kept him from ever meeting Steiner. When Steiner died on March 30, 1925,

Fritz was filled with remorse over having missed the opportunity to meet and talk with Steiner. He resolved to become thoroughly engaged in anthroposophic activity. He never stopped after this. Fritz turned a grievous mistake into a sterling quality.

Fritz and Bine, his wife, emigrated from Germany to the U.S. in 1929. Fritz was twenty-eight. His American English had a German accent mixed with a Cambridge pronunciation. At first it sounded a little stilted, but after you became accustomed to his pronunciation, it sounded distinctively Fritz. When he arrived at Bowdoin, he audited a course from fellow professors and continued auditing a course every semester for forty-two years. He laughed that he was the oldest, non-matriculating student in Bowdoin's history. There is the famous quotation from Chaucer on the steps of the Bowdoin Moulton Union, "And gladly wolde he lerne, and gladly teche" (Chaucer, *The Canterbury Tales,* General Prologue, line 310). This is a definition of the ideal teacher. Luckily, I had Fritz who loved to learn and teach.

Fritz walked into his first class in September of 1970. He had piercing blue eyes and a ruddy, choleric face that would become red when he was excited. He was about five feet seven inches tall, with the body of a short, offensive tackle, broad and stout. His blond hair had turned shocking white with age. He always wore a white shirt, tie with a tie clip, blue blazer, and grey pants. He carried an old black leather book bag, weighed down with books. He muttered to himself and opened the book bag. As he removed each book, he checked and affirmed that he had brought his intended books and delicately placed each one on a table. If you have ever seen a clown car in the circus, you might have wondered how so many clowns could fit into such a small car. Similarly, a dozen books emerged from Fritz's book bag. Fritz assembled a small library on the table next to his chair.

Fritz outlined the course. He spoke in a slow, evenly pitched voice that was very effective. "The title for this course, 'Friedriech Niezsche, A Problematic Thinker of Our Time,' is meant to make you ponder. Why is Nietzsche 'a problematic thinker'? I also hope to get Americans to pronounce Nietzsche the correct German way." Fritz then laughed and described the course requirements. "This is a senior seminar with limited enrollment. You are fortunate to have been selected. You must be prepared for class by thoroughly reading the literature. The class will be run as a seminar, and you are expected to engage actively in all discussions. If you do not participate, I will call on you, and it will affect your final grade. You will select a thesis and present it to me. After discussions with me, you will write this thesis into a paper of no less than twenty pages. After I read your thesis, you will then present your paper to the class. Is this understood?"

Fritz started reading *Thus Spake Zarathustra*. He found a translation that he thought was a little off. He picked up his German version, retranslated the words into English, and we were off and running. At first Fritz appeared difficult to follow. We all thought in a linear fashion, A, B, then C. Fritz led us through thoughts that seemed disconnected. After a few classes, it became apparent that we were not working hard enough to realize that all his digressions and tangents were directly connected with the theme. We were comfortable with linear thinking. Fritz operated with rhythmic thoughts that were more organic in nature. With Fritz you could almost see the thoughts evolving. They had the structure of a gyre or a spiral. Like a falcon, he circled an idea from various perspectives and then swooped down to make it his own. Fritz's approach from radically different perspectives would not abide a one-sided or dogmatic perspective. One of his constant phrases was, "Avoid dogma, avoid dogma." In contrast to dogmatism, Fritz espoused creativity. One of his favorite quotations from Goethe was "Each day anew." The longer Goethe quotation is insightful into Fritz's inner life: "This is the highest wisdom that I own; freedom and life are earned by those alone who conquer them each day anew" (*Faust II*).

Fritz had the amazing ability to listen to and address your question. He was dramatic and funny. He would make you feel that you were actually in the presence of Nietzsche, Hegel, Wagner, and other great thinkers. He would start to read an English translation, shake his head, and switch to the German, which might have some reference to a Latin or Greek quotation that he would also recite or read. He was totally engaged in the subject matter. He would act out certain scenes. During those vigorous lectures, he would literally work up a sweat.

During the seminar, Fritz expounded on Nietzsche's vision that Western civilization had gone into an intellectual and moral abyss and had lost its bearings. Reading and reciting Nietzsche with Fritz was like being in a thunderstorm with lightening and thunder all around and inside you. The thoughts were palpable. Nietzsche wrote dramatic scenes that engaged us, but whereas he presented the problem, Nietzsche did not offer a solution. Fritz hinted that the solution would come from another person. At the end of the last class he mentioned Rudolf Steiner and then ended the seminar, put his books into his book bag and left.

I was amazed that Fritz did not expound on Steiner, and I later went to his home to follow up. Fritz and Bine resided at 7 Page Street in Brunswick, which formed one of his favorite puns: "When in doubt, turn to Page 7." This invitation was given to thousands of Bowdoin students, and he meant it. I asked Fritz about Rudolf Steiner. He smiled, waved his index finger at me, and said, "Remember, you asked me that question." For the next fifteen years we discussed little else but Steiner. I asked why he did not teach a course on Steiner at Bowdoin. Fritz replied, "It cannot be done. Steiner is not an academic subject." He paused for effect. "But if a student would ask me to give a free seminar on Steiner, get a classroom, a day, and a time, I would consider it." I got the hint and asked Fritz if he would allow me to do so. He smiled and said yes.

The free seminar was an oral version of *Theosophy,* with Fritz describing humanity's spiritual nature. It was stunning in breadth and depth. Fritz did not use notes. He lived those thoughts; they were a natural progression for him, like a seed maturing into a plant. Sixty or more people attended his class on Steiner. Twelve people from my class of 220 students became involved in anthroposophic activity after graduation. He introduced hundreds to Rudolf Steiner, the founder of Waldorf schools and Anthroposophy. I have continued to read Steiner for forty-seven years.

Fritz was troubled that he should not have remained at Bowdoin, but should have gone to New York or a more anthroposophic locale. However, fate and karma intervened with his final class. Fritz basked in the number of young people who came at the end of his teaching career.

We became close friends, even thought Fritz was forty-eight years older than I. I would often visit his home. Fritz's study was a small library with shelves of books, a desk, photos, a couch, and a piano. Fritz playing the piano was the definition of choleric activity. He pounded the keys with joy and enthusiasm. This study became a *sanctum sanctorum,* where Fritz would have deep conversations. During a conversation on kamaloca, Fritz described how individuals must each purge their earthly desires upon entering the spiritual world. It would be painful to have unrequited, materialistic desires without a body to satisfy them. He stated that it was very similar to the concept of purgatory. He then asked me. "What would you desire after you have left your body? What would you miss the most?" I was about to say running, but thought he would not understand that desire. So I went to numbers two and three: "Chocolate chip cookies and vanilla ice cream." Fritz looked at me incredulously, shook his head, smiled kindly at my naiveté, and said, "Maybe this part will not be so hard for you."

Fritz covered a wide range of cultural and anthroposophic themes. For Fritz, Steiner's history of consciousness was an axiomatic understanding of humanity's evolution with all its fits and starts. His life experience gave him ample proof of Steiner's understanding. World War II was an especially hard time for Fritz and Bine. Many of their family and friends were trapped in Germany, persecuted by the Nazis, and had to survive during the final invasion of Germany. Whole cities were bombed into oblivion. Since many of their friends were Jewish and/or anthroposophists, Fritz and Bine were always on guard for news from Germany.

Fritz worked tirelessly to help his German friends. He was able to secure a teaching post for Walter Solmitz, who was so traumatized by his experiences in Dachau and World War II that he often contemplated suicide. Unfortunately, Walter did commit suicide in 1962. Fritz spoke at his friend's memorial service. "There was a quality in him that showed itself at the end of his life, sometimes to an unbearable degree. He felt the suffering of other people as his own suffering," Koelln said. "If this contributed greatly to his final total exhaustion, we must also remember that it was also the root of the great effect his deep personal concerns had on so many lives of his students and friends."

Fritz considered suicide to be a desperate answer and a violation of karmic rules. Fritz would immediately visit anyone who was contemplating suicide. Steiner had indicated that a person who committed suicide would have severe regrets in the afterlife and would have to constantly contemplate that act. Fritz said it was the equivalent of being in a claustrophobic jail. Steiner stated that a person would commit this act only once in the course of multiple incarnations.

Divorce is the other karmic issue that would get Fritz engaged. Fritz believed that love is the central activity of an individual's life. Fritz thought that marriage is sacred and one of the deepest karmic commitments a person can make. Vows were lifeblood to Fritz. Individuals were influenced by their future children to fall in love. Fritz would refer to the endless pictures of angels shooting arrows of love and desire, saying that although they seem simplistic, there is a grain of karmic truth in the images.

In one conversation, Fritz, the most profound person I have had the pleasure to meet, shocked me with the following statement: "The modern age tends toward superficiality. We are all superficial. Even I am superficial." I asked myself, "Wait, if Fritz is superficial, what does that make me? Super superficial?" Fritz believed that superficiality is deeply connected with the overwhelming materialism of modernity and denial of the spirit.

Fritz had experienced a minor bout with cancer. He thought our superficiality is manifested directly in our physical bodies as cancer and heart attacks. They are the major modern illnesses. Cancer cells are mutations of healthy cells with a meaningless replication and growth of cells without controls. The lack of controls overcomes the normal cell death. Heart attacks usually occur when a blood clot blocks blood flow to the heart. Without blood, tissue loses oxygen and dies. For Fritz, the modern dilemma of being incapable of loving anyone but ourselves (i.e., immense egotism) is not a metaphor. Our egotism blocks the flow of love. It is the heart that suffers this for us. It is an abundantly clear observation. Similarly, the organs suffer cancer because of our superficial addiction to shiny things.

Fritz suffered from an addiction to cigarettes. When he finally quit, went cold turkey, and won the battle, he said it was the hardest thing he had ever done. He said he stopped when he felt "the cigarettes were smoking him."

Fritz had an accurate understanding of modern times, but that did not prevent him from making fun of it or himself. A small child once saw Fritz on the street and, with wide eyes, asked, "Are you Santa Claus?" Fritz did not miss a beat. "Yes, I am." The child was delighted. Fritz stated that every human being has three bodies: physical, etheric, and astral, but that Americans have four: physical, etheric, astral, and a car! Fritz thought that he was not a completely modern person because he never learned to drive a car. He and Bine lived a few minutes walk from Bowdoin College and walked to the market, stores, and church.

Although Fritz was not Catholic, he understood Catholicism and the inherent beauty of the Mass and communion. He once asked me, "Why did you stop using Latin in the Mass?" He asked me as if it had been my decision. I replied with the standard post-Vatican II response: "No one speaks Latin anymore; no one knows what is going on in the Mass. Therefore, why not switch to the vernacular and increase comprehension?" Fritz replied, "The cultus of transubstantiation has been in Latin for nearly two thousand years. You should never have lost a living connection with the language and the cultus. It is still real, but not as powerful as when it maintained the original language."

I told Fritz about an intense dream.

I dreamed of a steel fence, tall and black with points at the top. Behind the fence was a green lawn, verdant and tranquil.

Off in the distant, left-hand corner of the field, the sun shined brightly.

I walked to the fence to gaze at the sun, which seemed to transform itself into a lamb. My hands rested on the cold steel fence. I became engrossed and wanted to get closer as the lamb started to turn into a cross.

Out of the corner of my eye, I noticed a small man in a majestic, long blue robe walking, or rather floating, down the left side of the fence. He turned the corner where the two sides joined into a right angle. He approached me, but my attention was on the transformation of the lamb into a cross.

I was so engrossed that I parted the steel bars as if they were butter. I stared at the cross and started to step through the bars. Just as I had demonstrated immense strength, the little man came up to my right side and touched my right elbow. It was as if he had a magnet. He moved me away from the fence and started to talk to me. His speech was incomprehensible. His blue gown was decorated with archaic symbols. I was totally confused and felt uneasy. He walked to my left side and continued to speak.

Finally, I asked, "But how do I know that you are a Christian?" With that, the first finger of his right hand pointed to his left hand. He raised the ring finger on his left hand. On this finger was the figure of a fish. With that I felt immense relief and continued to walk with him.

I rarely shared these intense dreams with friends, because it usually led to silence. No one knew how to react, but not Fritz. He looked at me and said, "You could have died that night." Now he had my full attention. "When you separated the bars, you may have been about to leave this physical world, but you were stopped. This sometimes happens to an individual. One goes for a walk and at the last minute, abruptly and seemingly for no logical reason, makes a left instead of a right at a corner, and bricks fall where one would have walked." I realized that I was in the presence of an advanced soul who had a deep understanding of life.

Bowdoin was just becoming coeducational; the students there were all male until 1970. Fritz and Bine had three daughters and no sons. However, if you were connected with Fritz, you became one of "Fritz's boys." It was a mark of honor in our anthroposophic circles. It meant that one had the good karma of attending Bowdoin and encountering this amazing man.

One of Fritz's favorite questions was to ask Bowdoin seniors what they wanted after graduation. Fritz was stunned that most answered with a Hallmark kind of superficiality. The most common answer was "I want to be happy." Fritz would then respond, "Oh boy, do *you* have a lot to learn." For Fritz, happiness is the byproduct of a meaningful life, not a goal.

Fritz had boundless zest for life. This was most evident in his love of food and eating. When Fritz and Bine left for a cruise to Europe after his retirement from Bowdoin College, a number of Fritz's boys went to the boat to wish them bon voyage. Fritz, of course, invited us to eat and talk with him. Fritz was able to speak eloquently, devour vast amounts of food, and order another platter from the waiter, all at the same time. He never missed a beat. Bine would say demurely, "I can't eat any more." This was their code for Fritz to take Bine's portion and eat that, too.

This all occurred in the midst of Fritz's description of how he was teaching two courses on the boat: Introductory Italian for those who did not speak Italian—"That way, their experience will be richer in Italy"—and, ever practical, a course on how to avoid seasickness.

Fritz later taught at Emerson College in England, where I visited him. One day we were walking to Emerson College, and Fritz asked me a question: "Two men—an old man like me and a young man like you—were walking together to a train station. The old man was carrying heavy luggage. The young man had no luggage. Who gets there first?" I answered the young man. Fritz smiled and asked, "What part of *together* do you not understand?"

Fritz had the unique ability to judge how much of a complex idea someone could understand. He would go up to that point and not beyond the individual's capacity. He could also remember where the last conversation had left off and proceed from there, even after a hiatus of weeks or months.

After retiring from Bowdoin at seventy, Fritz taught a three-week class on Goethe at the Kimberton Waldorf School, where I taught. He stayed with my wife and me in our home. Each dinnertime was an advanced course in Christology, Western Literature, Philosophy, and Anthroposophy. He continued to do this post-retirement until he was seventy-seven.

One of the lasting images I have of Fritz is when we were standing outside the Kimberton Waldorf School. Two young girls were waiting to be picked up by their mother after school. They were turning graceful cartwheels on the grass. Fritz looked at them, smiled, and stated, "I can't wait to come back and do that again!"

Fritz was asked to translate Steiner's *Riddles of Philosophy* into English. His introduction is one of the best summaries of Steiner I have ever read.

Rudolf Steiner's *Riddles of Philosophy: Presented in an Outline of Its History* is not a history of philosophy in the usual sense of the word. It does not give a history of the philosophical systems, nor does it present a number of philosophical problems historically. Its real concern touches on something deeper than this, on riddles rather than problems. Philosophical concepts, systems, and problems are, to be sure, to be dealt with in this book. But it is not *their* history that is to be described here. Where they are discussed they become symptoms rather than the objects of the search. The search itself wants to reveal a process that is overlooked in the usual history of philosophy. It is the mysterious process in which philosophical thinking appears in human history. Philosophical thinking as it is here meant is known only in Western civilization. Oriental philosophy has its origin in a different kind of consciousness, and it is not to be considered in this book.

What is new here is the treatment of the history of philosophic thinking as a manifestation of the evolution of human consciousness. Such a treatment requires a fine sense of observation. Not merely the thoughts must be observed, but behind them the thinking in which they appear.

To follow Steiner in his subtle description of the process of the metamorphosis of this thinking in the history of philosophy we should remember he sees the human consciousness in an evolution. It has not always been what it is now, and what it is now it will not be in the future. This is a fundamental concept of Anthroposophy. The metamorphosis of the consciousness is not only described in Steiner's anthroposophic books but in a number of them directions are given from which we can learn to participate in this transformation actively. This is explicitly done not only in his *Knowledge of the Higher Worlds,* but also in certain chapters of his books *Theosophy* and *An Outline of Occult Science,* as well as several of his other books on Anthroposophy.

The objection may be raised at this point that the application of concepts derived from spiritual exercises is not admissible in a field of pure philosophical studies, where every concept used should be clearly comprehensible without any preconceived ideas. Steiner's earlier philosophical books did not seem to imply any such presuppositions and his anthroposophic works therefore appear to mark a definite departure from his earlier philosophical ones.

It is indeed significant that the anthroposophic works appear only after a long period of philosophic studies. A glance at Rudolf Steiner's bibliography shows that it is only after twenty years of philosophical studies that his Anthroposophy as a science of the spirit appears on the scene. The purely philosophical publications begin with his *Introductions to Goethe's Natural Scientific Writings* (1883–97) and with the *Fundamental Outline of a Theory of Knowledge Implicit in Goethe's World Conception* (1886). They are followed by his own theory of knowledge presented in *Truth and Knowledge* in 1892 and his *Philosophy of Freedom* (also translated as *Philosophy of Spiritual Activity*) of 1894. This work presents clearly the climax of Steiner's philosophy, and it should be studied carefully by anyone who intends to arrive at a valid judgment of his later Anthroposophy. It is, however, still several years before the books appear that contain the result of his spiritual science. Not only his book *Friedrich Nietzsche: Fighter for Freedom* (1895) and *Goethe's World Conception* (1897), but also his *World- and Life-Conceptions of the Nineteenth Century* (1900), and even his *Mystics at the Dawn of the Modern Age and Their Relation to the Current Natural–Scientific Paradigm* (1901), could have been understood as merely historical descriptions.

With Steiner's next work we seem to enter an entirely different world. *Christianity as Mystical Fact and the Mysteries of Antiquity* clearly begin the series of his distinctly anthroposophic works. Like *Theosophy* (1904), his *Knowledge of the Higher Worlds and its Attainment* (1905/08) and his *Occult Science* (1910), it could have been written only by an occultist who spoke from a level of consciousness that one did not have to assume as the source of his earlier books.

To the casual reader it could appear that there was a distinct break in Steiner's world conception at the beginning of the century, and this is also the conclusion drawn by some of his critics.

Rudolf Steiner's own words, however, as well as a study of both phases of his work, leave no doubt that there was no such break in his world conception. He clearly states that knowledge derived from a higher level of consciousness was always at his disposal, also at the time of his early philosophical publications. His deep concern was the question: How could one speak about worlds not immediately accessible to scarcely anybody else in an age in which materialism and agnosticism ruled without any serious opposition. He found both so deeply rooted in Western civilization that he had to ask himself at times: Will it always be necessary to keep entirely silent about this higher knowledge.

In this time he turned to the study of representative thinkers of his time and of the more recent past in whose conceptions of world and life he now penetrated to experience their depth and their limitations. In Goethe's world he found the leverage to overcome the basic agnosticism and materialism to which the age had surrendered. In Nietzsche he saw the tragic figure who had been overpowered by it and whose life was broken by the fact that his spiritual sensitivity made it impossible for him to live in this world and his intellectual integrity forbade him to submit to what he had to consider as the dishonest double standard of his time.

Neither Rudolf Steiner's Nietzsche book nor his writings on Goethe's conception of the world are meant to be merely descriptive accounts of philosophical systems or problems. They reveal an inner struggle of the spirit that is caused by the spiritual situation of their time and in which the reader must share to follow these books with a full understanding. When these studies are then extended to comprise longer periods of time as in the *World and Life Conceptions of the Nineteenth Century* and in *Mysticism at the Dawn of the Modern Age* soul conditions under which the individual thinkers have had to work to become more and more visible.

When Rudolf Steiner published the present work in 1914 as *The Riddles of Philosophy* he used the book *World- and Life-Conception of the Nineteenth Century* as part two, which is now preceded by an outline of the entire history of philosophy in the Western world.

At this time Steiner's anthroposophic books had appeared in which the evolution of human consciousness plays an important role. It could now be partly demonstrated in an outline of the philosophical thinking of the Western world.

Rudolf Steiner's approach to history is symptomatological, and it is this method that he also applies to the history of philosophy. The thoughts developed in the course of this history are treated as symptomatic facts for the mode of thinking prevalent in a given time. He sees four distinct phases in the course of Western thought evolution. They are periods of seven to eight centuries each, beginning with the pre-Socratic thinkers in Greece.

Here pure thought as such, free of images, develops out of an older form of consciousness that is expressed in myths and symbolic pictures. It reaches its climax in the classical philosophies of Socrates, Plato, and Aristotle, and ends with the Hellenistic period.

A second phase begins with Christianity and reaches as far as the ninth century AD. This time, Rudolf Steiner characterizes as the age of the awakening self-consciousness, and he is convinced that an intense historical study of this period will more and more prove the adequacy of that term. The emergence of a greater self-awareness at this time diminishes the importance of conceptional thinking as the religious concern of the soul with its own destiny grows. The emerging self-consciousness of this phase is intensely felt, but does not lead to an intellectual occupation with the concept of this *"self."* In a third period a new concern becomes prevalent when the scholastic philosophers become more and more confronted with the tormenting question of the reality of thought itself. What is often regarded as an aberration into mere verbal quarrels, the medieval discussions of the significance of the universal concepts, is now seen as a soul struggle of a profound human concern. Thus the long war between Realism and Nominalism appears in a new light. As the nominalists seem to emerge more and more as the victors the thought climate for the fourth phase is gradually prepared.

Since the Renaissance, natural science proceeds to develop a world conception in which the self-conscious ego must experience itself as a foreign element. The emergence of this experience leads to a new inner struggle in which the fourth phase of the history of philosophy is from now on deeply engaged in its predominant thought currents: It is the phase of consciousness in which we still live. The various forms of idealistic, materialistic, and agnostic philosophies are subject to the tension caused by the indicated situation. As Steiner characterizes them he points out that the different thinker personalities can be quite unconscious of the currents that manifest themselves in their thinking although their ideas and thought combinations receive direction and form from them.

In the last chapter of the second part of the book Steiner describes his own philosophy as he had developed it in his earlier books *Truth and Science* and *Philosophy of Freedom*. In this description the relation between his philosophical works and his anthroposophic ones also becomes clear. As a philosophy of spiritual activity, the *Philosophy of Freedom* had not merely given an analysis of the factors involved in the process of knowledge, nor had the possibility of human freedom within a world apparently determined on all sides merely been logically shown. What the study of this book meant to supply was at the same time a course of concentrated exercise of thinking that was to develop a new power through which man really *becomes* free. As Aristotle's statement (Metaph. XII, 7) that *the actuality of thinking is life* in this way becomes a real experience of the thinker, human freedom is born. Man becomes free in his actions in the external world, developing the moral imagination necessary for the situation in which he finds himself. At the same time his spirit frees itself from the bodily encasement in which thoughts had appeared as unreal shadows. The process of his real spiritual development has begun.

In this way the *Riddles of Philosophy* may be considered as a bridge that can lead from Steiner's early philosophical works into the study of Anthroposophy. The undercurrents characterized in the four main phases of the evolution of thought lead from potentiality to ever increasing actuality of the awakening spirit. And for the exercises described in the specific anthroposophic books there can be no better preparation than the concentrated study of Rudolf Steiner's *Philosophy of Spiritual Activity.*

Fritz C. A. Koelln
Bowdoin College
Brunswick, Maine
April 1973 (pp. vii–xii)

†

For those of us who were lucky enough to study with Fritz, the last sentence of the preceding text rings like a clarion bell. For Fritz, *The Philosophy of Freedom* was the quintessential work by Steiner, one with which students of Steiner have to wrestle. In doing such, each individual could self-ignite the process of spiritual activity. Fritz stated a concentrated study; he was exact in his rigorous study of Steiner. Fritz's summary of Steiner's major opus is excellent: "What the study of this book meant to supply was at the same time a course of concentrated exercise of thinking that was to develop a new power through which the human being *becomes* truly free."

He once suggested that I read *Knowledge of the Higher Worlds*. I was a philosophy major and had read Hegel and Kant. How hard could this book be? I started reading the work, and I felt as if I were running in cement. The next time I met with Fritz, he asked me about my reading. I was embarrassed to admit that it took me more than three weeks. Fritz smiled at me and said, "Bine and I read it one paragraph at a time every night before we fall asleep. We read it back and forth to one another ten times." One paragraph at a time! I would have never thought of such a reading. It made me realize that Fritz was not reading; he was meditating upon each and every paragraph. He was making each paragraph an experience. He was making it his own spiritual experience.

When Fritz was in his eighties, he once walked me to the back of his home, where carpenters were building shelves in a back room. Fritz said, "This is the room where I am going to die." There was no bed yet, just shelves. "These shelves will have my favorite three thousand books so I don't have to go up or down steps." These favorite books were his friends and companions during life, and he wanted to visit them again and again.

Fritz experienced ideas as living realities, not as dead concepts. He suggested trying on an idea as you would a jacket and walk around in it for a while. If it fits, keep it. If not, discard it. Fritz thought of reincarnation as a Christian idea. We are given an opportunity to amend our previous transgressions and to improve our Christlike nature. To Fritz it was hubris to assume we could do this in one lifetime.

Two of Fritz's grandchildren were children with special needs who luckily were part of a Camphill community. To see how this scholarly man and his wife lovingly interacted with their grandchildren was all you needed to see to understand Christian kindness. Fritz and Bine stated that those children were a gift, and that the children sacrificially incarnated to bring love to the Koelln family and to the world.

Finding four-leaf clovers was a special skill that Fritz practiced everywhere. He said you just had to wait and look for them, and they would make themselves known. You would often find Fritz staring at the ground, seemingly in deep thoughts or meditation or just lost. He was actually hunting for four-leaf clovers.

Fritz's kindness extended to people he had never met. When my son Kevin was born, Fritz and Bine wrote him a birth greeting card that included a four-leaf clover. Here are his and Bine's words of greeting to a newborn child. It reads almost as if from a fairytale or a myth.

Dear little Kevin,

Thank you for coming to live your earthly life with mother Linda, father Neill, and sister Nicole, and all others who will love you. May you be blessed with all the blessings heaven has in store for you. And may you be a blessing for everyone else who comes your way.

We wish that your dear mother will recover soon from giving birth to you, and also thank your dear father very much for announcing unto us your happy arrival. We rejoice with them.

With love to you and your dear family.

Fritz and Bine Koelln

Bruce Murphy once attended a Fritz lecture and sat near Hans Pusch, Fritz's dear old boyhood and anthroposophic friend, with whom he grew up in Hamburg. Both Hans and Bruce were amazed by Fritz's dramatic lecture. Hans stated that watching Fritz grow over the years reminded him of the old joke in *The New Yorker* about two rabbits walking in New York City and looking through a Saks Fifth Avenue window at a mannequin wearing a beautiful rabbit coat and saying, "Look at what we can become!"

Fritz was Michaelic. He was not afraid of confronting evil. At one point he stated, "Your generation is very brave!" I had always thought the opposite—that my generation was weak and lacked grit. I looked puzzled. Fritz immediately started talking of how before we are born we view the world and its environs as we are incarnating. Fritz said that to see the darkness of World War I, World War II, and the Holocaust demanded brave souls who still wanted to incarnate. He then said that one had to be brave to be born into a modern world that was so spiritually dark. He became emphatic: "You must carry the light through the darkness, no matter how dark it becomes. Always carry the light. I wish I could be here with you in the coming trials. Always carry the light and protect it."

Steiner states in *The Philosophy of Freedom*, "Idealists *revel* spiritually in the transformation of their ideals into reality" (p. 198). Fritz reveled.

John Fentress Gardner

John Fentress Gardner

"Who has more obedience than I masters me..."

EMERSON, *Self-reliance*

John F. Gardner was born July 3, 1912 in San Acacio, Colorado. He was admitted to Princeton College at the age of fifteen and also attended Rollins College, where he met his future wife, Carol Hemingway. In 1933, he was introduced to the work of Rudolf Steiner, which he took up with great enthusiasm during a four- month stay at the Goetheanum in Dornach, Switzerland. That same year, without the consent of Carol's brother Ernest Hemingway, he and Carol were married. John rejected the lure of fame that Ernest represented, and Ernest, on his side, never spoke to his youngest sister again.

John participated in biodynamic farming while looking after psychiatric patients. During World War II, he served as a Navy corpsman in a hospital he helped build as a Seabee on Guam. Following the war, he worked on graduate studies at Teachers College, Columbia University. His thesis was titled *The Freeing of Education from the Political Sphere of the State.* He was a fervent advocate of freedom, hence his concern about the state controlling education. This theme would become a constant throughout his life.

He became faculty chair at the Waldorf school of Garden City, New York, where he helped build the school for children from pre-school through twelfth grade, adding buildings along the way. From

1964 to '78, he directed the Waldorf Institute for Liberal Education in conjunction with Adelphi University. At his retirement, the university awarded him an honorary doctorate of letters. He was a lecturer and writer on education, spirituality, and America, producing his books *American Heralds of the Spirit: Emerson, Whitman, and Melville* (1991); *Education in Search of the Spirit: Essays on American Education* (1996); and *Youth Longs to Know: Explorations of the Spirit in Education* (1997). He was also a lifelong student and interpreter of Rudolf Steiner, whose *Calendar of the Soul* he translated.

He went to the other side on July 7, 1998, in the Buckley Nursing Home in Greenfield, Massachusetts. He was eighty-six.

I first met John Gardner in May of 1972. I had just returned from Emerson College in Sussex, England, after visiting professor Fritz Koelln, my beloved teacher from Bowdoin College, who first introduced me to Anthroposophy. At Emerson College, I had decided to apply to the Waldorf Institute at Adelphi University in Garden City, Long Island. Professor Koelln was very enthusiastic about my application to the institute and teaching in a Waldorf school. He gave me a slight grin and said, "Maybe you can make John Gardner laugh a little. He is too serious and somber. You can lighten him up."

Since John was faculty chair at the Waldorf school and ran the Master's program in conjunction with Adelphi University, he was exceptionally busy. I had to wait for several minutes outside his office for my admission interview for the Waldorf Institute Master's Program. He appeared almost embarrassed and cordially invited me into his office. After he asked me my name, we sat in silence for a while. He was a tall, lean man with striking blue eyes and an exceptionally high forehead. You would not miss him in a crowd.

His thinking was as clear as a cloudless, Rocky Mountain sky. And equally American!

We continued to sit in silence in his office. The interview turned into a Quaker meeting where silence is honored. Then he asked a few perfunctory questions. "Where did you go to college?" "What was your major?" Finally I thought it would help my cause to mention visiting Professor Koelln at Emerson College. John then casually asked me what I thought of Emerson College.

Foolish young man that I was, I stated exactly what I thought of Emerson College: "A bit effete for me." In later years, I grew to realize that leading with such a statement was impolite and downright dangerous. But John lit up like a Christmas tree. He stated, "I know exactly what you mean. How did you come to that observation?" I said that a number of my friends from Bowdoin had gone there and within a few days started speaking a form of English that was unheard at Bowdoin. It reminded me of Percy Bysshe Shelley. I called it the Emersonian twang. John laughed out loud. The interview was basically over. I got up to leave and inquired about a scholarship. John asked me how much I needed. I figured out a number and stated it. John said fine, and we were done. My kind of guy!

It is no coincidence that he was born a day before Independence Day and died a few days after. John was a walking embodiment of independence. He was his own man and a distinct individuality. John was a dedicated student of Rudolf Steiner and had a deep knowledge of Steiner's works. More important, John had made these thoughts his own. His thinking, feeling, and willing were affected directly by his lifelong study of Steiner. His favorite authors promoted the inherent sanctity of each individual and the quest for freedom: Steiner, Emerson, Melville, and Whitman. For an exhilarating adventure with the last three writers, read John's essays in his book *American Heralds of the Spirit*.

Starting in September 1972, twenty of us attended classes with John and Lee Lecraw on Waldorf pedagogy and techniques. John emphasized rigorous, clear thinking, especially as demonstrated by Rudolf Steiner in *The Philosophy of Freedom*. He would invite you into his exploration of Steiner's insights. It was an intellectual tour de force. John had wrestled with those thoughts for decades, and they had become his best friends. Each chapter was a jewel that would shine with his understanding. This went beyond teacher-and-student; it was more like Socrates-as-midwife to ideas. Individuals of the most varied abilities and temperaments could partake on an equal footing. It was like running with a supremely gifted runner who floated instead of straining. By following his pace, one covered more ground and maintained the correct balance and breathing. It was not leading in the conventional, pedantic style of the Academy; it was seeking and finding the truth in a collaborative, artistic way. Epiphanies were in evidence.

We had an experience of knowledge similar to what Steiner describes:

> Only when I follow my love for my objective is it I myself who acts. I act, at this level of morality not because I acknowledge a lord over me or an external authority or a so-called inner voice; I acknowledge no external principle for my action, because I have found in myself the ground for my action— namely, my love of the action. I do not work out mentally whether my action is good or bad; I carry it out because I love it. My action will be "good" if my intuition, steeped in love, finds its right place within the intuitively experience-able world continuum; it will be "bad" if this is not the case. Again, I do not ask myself, "How would someone else act in

my position?" I act as I, this particular individuality, find I have occasion to do. No general usage, no common custom, no maxim applying to everyone, no moral standard is my immediate guide, but my love for the deed. I feel no compulsion—neither the compulsion of nature that guides me through my instincts nor the compulsion of the moral commandments, but I want simply to carry out what lies within me. (*The Philosophy of Freedom*, pp. 135–36)

This man who had a deserved reputation as a disciplinarian was most concerned about freedom and love! John knew that to experience spiritual freedom and spiritual love one needed to be a disciple to truth and to master self-control. John assiduously worked on self-knowledge. This effort radiated through him to many who encountered him. John's spiritual activity was a spark that ignited other people in his presence. He gladly shared the fruits of his spiritual activity.

John had a unique ability to find teachers. He would look for light in a person's eyes and then he would fan that flame. He could size up a potential teacher and help the person mature into a model teacher; he was a teacher of teachers.

John could use light humor at someone's expense. He would use his wit to get you back on track. At one point I had annoyed my Waldorf Institute classmates with too many sarcastic jokes. They complained, and John commented, "You have to forgive Neill; he is not quite housebroken yet." Laughter ensued.

It was immensely enjoyable to catch him when he made a mistake. John was a good actor and would often make his point by enacting it with his facial gestures or body movements. He once started to discuss foolish nervousness and, as an example, used runners before a hundred-yard dash. John gesticulated wildly with his arms and tried to mimic runners before a race. John had stumbled into one of the few areas where I had more experience and knowledge than he did. I pounced. "While it is partially correct that runners are nervous before a race, they are also trying to keep their limbs loose before maximum exertion." I really wanted to start the statement with "Wrong," but I restrained myself.

He was a manifestation of Emerson's statement, which he frequently quoted, "Who has more obedience than I masters me, though he should not raise his finger. Round him I must revolve by the gravitation of spirits" (Emerson, *Self-reliance*). Such discipline was evident in his walk. John strode with a refined but purposeful ease. It was also apparent in his posture. John never slouched. He was present and accounted for. John had little interest in small talk and was concerned with matters of consequence. This could be uncomfortable for some people. You did not ask John what he thought of the Knicks or Giants sport teams. But this never affected his incredible civility. He could be brusque or make mistakes, and when he made them they were big! But he was consistently authentic.

John understood that a leader serves the higher good of the group. This demands discipline and the denial of self-serving egotism by both the leader and the group. The leader should seek to serve the ideal of the group by offering his service in humility. This is in direct contrast to the modern misunderstanding of leadership, whereby the largest ego becomes the boss and everyone else just follows orders. Since John had a strong personality, it would be easy to think he ran the show. However, anyone who has met the teachers with whom John worked and saw what distinct individuals they were would quickly understand how erroneous such a misunderstanding is.

John's leadership was more like a conductor than a quarterback. He was aligned to the musical score and helped individuals realize their greatest potential. He did not dictate; he educated in the sense of *educere*—leading forth and nurturing. John had immense trust in each individual. There were numerous times when he gave advice, he would end with "Do what you think is best."

Since John was so self-disciplined, his discipline could unfortunately intimidate others. Some felt that they were being judged. Rather, John was determined to lead a conscious life and he constantly worked on himself to achieve that daily goal. He set a high bar for himself and you felt it in his presence. Because John took thinking very seriously, he assumed you would also. If you were not a serious thinker, John could state your position better than you could. John also understood the direct connection between morality and spiritual activity. Since he took Steiner's ideas seriously, ideas such as "For every one step you take in the pursuit of higher knowledge, take three steps in the perfection of your own character" (Steiner, *Knowledge of the Higher Worlds*, p. 69) were imperatives for him. His moral rectitude was readily evident. This intimidated some individuals. They felt John was judgmental, almost authoritarian. Like most human beings, John was only dimly aware of how he impacted other human beings. Others flourished in his rigor.

Discipline by itself is an empty practice. John, especially in his later years, grew into a devotional practice centered on Christ. This jarred some, who expected John to maintain his previous personal traits all the way to his death. To others, this growth was the perfect accomplishment of his later life. John continued to grow and to work on himself until his last breath.

When John first taught at the Rudolf Steiner School in New York City, he was amazed that no one spoke to the parents about Rudolf Steiner, Anthroposophy, or Waldorf education. At the Garden City Waldorf School, John regularly met with parents to increase their understanding of the school's philosophy. John did it in a way that translated Steiner, Anthroposophy, and Waldorf pedagogy into the American culture and vernacular.

Even though he was an excellent speaker, John did not like to lecture. He wanted to promote spiritual activity. He wanted each individual to be engaged and participating in the act of self-discovery. John was an active gardener and made compost continuously to enrich his plants. He would compare thinking and meeting as composting ideas. He would take what might appear to be refuse and turn it into the essential element. At the end of his life, he had eight compost piles around his property.

John was at his best in study groups and in his writings. He could quickly summarize the essence or, as he would say, the "nub" of an idea. John could get a group to think in concert. He would ask individuals for their ideas, and he would bring those seemingly disparate ideas into a whole. There was no set agenda. It was addressing the ideas that were manifested in the group. These meetings were both planned in that John had often contemplated these ideas and spontaneous, in that he nurtured each individual to bring forth ideas in that exact moment.

John was a master of conducting discussions. Like a conductor, he would stand in front of a group. He would then ask simple, yet profound questions, such as, "What concerns you?" Individuals would raise their hands and suggest various topics, ideas, and problems, from the educational to the political, to the spiritual realms. John would summarize them and write them on a blackboard. He would not judge them in any way. He would often pause, and extended periods of silence would follow. One knew he was listening intently. He would ask a person to clarify a point. Then with a blackboard full of ideas, he would start to group them and find common themes. He would eliminate the nonessential and circle the essential. He would weave the essential points together in an artistic creation. He would often ask a person if two ideas seemed connected. It was a communal effort or, as Marjorie Spock so clearly defined it, a "Goethean conversation."

He never backed away from a challenging question and always answered with candor, as well as insight. He was always in the present. What John brought was his presence. His presence was a manifestation of both lucid intellect and *Gemüt*, or heartfelt thinking. Ideas became alive and were quickened. The result was exhilarating. One felt, *Yes, this is an example of sense-free thinking.* This sense-free thinking is at the core of Steiner's *The Philosophy of Freedom* where Steiner boldly invites the reader to experience a thinking that is not bound to the senses and is manifested in imagination, inspiration, and intuition.

John was an artist, a creative artist in the realm of ideas as described in Steiner's 1918 revised preface to his *Philosophy of Freedom:*

> All real philosophers have been *artists in concepts.* For them, human ideas have become artistic materials, and scientific methods have become artistic technique. Thereby, abstract thinking attains concrete, individual life. Ideas become powers of life. Then we not merely know about things, but have made knowing into a real, self-governing organism. Our active, real consciousness has lifted itself above mere passive reception of truths. (ibid., p. xxx)

John's meetings created a vessel. Each individual made an effort and a sacrifice to participate in the group. This allowed the spiritual world to bless the meeting and shower grace upon the attendees. "Where two or more are gathered in my name there am I with them" (Matt. 18:20).

To balance his serious nature, John did have a sense of humor and could laugh and make fun of himself. On our last day at the Waldorf Institute, we put on a short skit. Jason played John. Jason had mastered John's signature movements from cleaning the table of invisible dust with the sweep of his hand to summarizing a point by compressing his fingers into the nub of a point. Debbie played Ann and had the electric efficiency and smarts that Ann displayed. The conversation was about an applicant to the institute, Bob, who was waiting outside. Bob came in, and there was John's usual silence. I was playing a statue of Rudolf Steiner. I was behind John, and after John's long silence, I came alive only to his sight. I whispered profound questions into John's ear, such as, "Ask him his name." John would do so. Then, "Ask him where he went to college." At this point John and Lee Lecraw were laughing so hard that their eyes were filled with tears. John said at the end of the skit. "Well, I am glad we are graduating you today!"

John always helped others, and his door was always open. A wide range of people came to him for guidance. John firmly understood Rudolf Steiner's central mission for Anthroposophy is to prepare for the second coming of Christ, which began in 1933. John also understood that individuals would want to incarnate to be near the Christ, and that the incarnation of more gifted individuals would increase around the middle of the twentieth century. John understood Steiner's statement that we are all clairvoyants, but that we just don't know it yet.

John was always nurturing the spiritual gifts of individuals. He thought that a Waldorf school should be a spiritual home in just that sense for teachers and students alike. Waldorf pedagogy was developed by Rudolf Steiner to foster the appropriate incarnation of children into this complex, materialistic world.

Often in the Bible, when a spiritual event occurs, Christ soothed people and stated, "Fear not." There is a reason for this constant refrain. It is because we are accustomed to sense-bound reality. Sense-free reality can be unnerving and frightening. Ironically, people who are interested in a spiritual life can become unhinged by what they aspire for, because the spirit is often not what we projected it would be. The spirit is fluid and nonlinear. It is based on growth not death. Most of us are fine with physical reality, but if we are not careful we can become confused and imbalanced with spiritual activity.

Personalities, egos, and karma always come into play with groups, even with the kindest group of people. Actually that is exactly the target for the devil—to break up a solid community gives him joy. And he is endlessly brilliant at it.

John, like all of us, made mistakes. He could be cold. He had a very strong view of himself and always knew where he stood. Yet he could also be his own sternest critic; he expected much of everyone, especially himself. Extremely intelligent and well read, he was no one's fool. He lived Steiner's thoughts on a daily basis, especially *The Philosophy of Freedom*. It is easy to see how some individuals could be put off or offended by a profound man who always discussed matters of consequence. He was transparent. A colleague once said to me that what he admired most about John was that his faults were immediately evident. John did not hide them. They were front and center. Many leaders lack integrity and act as if they have no flaws. For some reason, certain people thought John had to be perfect. John had an arrogant side, but show me a person who is not a sinner. We are all imperfect.

Rudolf Steiner clearly stated numerous times that gifted individuals would incarnate with distinct spiritual gifts, and that they are a blessing to humanity. However, since they are gifted they might not fit into a secular, materialistic world and would need to find kind souls to help them incarnate into the modern world.

At one point a young man who was an alumnus of the Waldorf high school and a college graduate approached John with unusual issues. John was willing to work with the young man and help him with his issues. He gave him a job in the Waldorf Press and then admitted him into the institute. John understood that the young man had spiritual insight. The key to spirituality is balance. When we lose our balance, we can go off in a million inappropriate directions. John's grounded nature made him a good stabilizer for such a young man.

When John started to become public with this young man's capabilities and insights, he underestimated the reaction of his colleagues. The depth of the fear they felt was unsettling, and John did not address it sufficiently—nor perhaps with the degree of compassion required to restore harmony and calm. They did not understand what had happened to John's former way of being. Previously John had frowned upon rock music. This thoroughly modern young man played the piano and had an electric keyboard. He played intuitively improvised music, not rock—a fact that is more important than it should be, but a reflection of the hysteria at the time. It infuriated several people that he used to do this in the morning in the small gym with John.

In Waldorf, "no rock and roll" had been a core belief. John had done too good a job at creating a taboo against rock and roll. The high school faculty then decided that this position on rock was not working. The young man later agreed with this, but the decision was made in the high school faculty meeting before he reappeared in the school and without consultation with him—or John. The idea was to have a dinner and dance and take the sting out of the music. However this was conflated as John and the young man's idea.

The irony is that a free thinker needs to set up standards to create a viable community. However, a free thinker cannot be constrained by preconceived ideas. A leader must be creative, an artist.

This transformation in John's thinking troubled many, though not all, of his friends and colleagues. Prior to working with the young man, John had explored a direct approach to the spiritual world, especially as expressed by some Christian charismatic authors. As head of the several Steiner study groups, his attempts to deepen the reverential dimensions of Anthroposophy disturbed some people, choosing to think he was abandoning Anthroposophy. However, he felt he was deepening his embrace of its essence. This was probably a larger issue than that of rock and roll, but John's issues and buried resentments were all secondary to the terror of the Spirit. People thought John was under the misguided influence of that young man and were worried for him and the school's future, a fear brought about largely in self-fulfilling hysteria. Although John was no longer its faculty chair or even a faculty member, his presence was influential. All these misunderstandings led to a major conflagration of friend against friend. The school lost its balance; the center did not hold.

John never wavered amid all the confusion and conflict—and the outrageously false attacks against him. He did not counter-attack or lose his cool. Looking back on these events in later years, John faulted himself for not having been sufficiently empathetic and loving amid this strife. The positive side of this is that he remained composed and calm when very few could have maintained that composure.

Many inaccurate statements were expressed about John—he had lost his marbles, or he had fallen under the spell of that young man.

I often met, spoke with, and wrote to John. He was still the clear thinker he'd always been. He was not evil or feeble.

This led to a traumatic time where John had to decide whether to support the work of the young man or cease and desist—even expel him from the institute as some of the faculty and a number of aroused parents wanted him to do. It was an impasse. After deep prayer and meditation, John decided he could not remain at the school if it could not come to terms with this young person. He left twenty-five years of work, which included building and leading a school. His decision ignited the departure of nearly a third of the teachers. Some chose to leave through principle, while others were forced out. The school was rocked to its core. Parents and students were duly concerned, and just about everyone was confused. Spiritual activity is not without its consequences, and it is the reason Christ says, "Fear not."

Life is filled with pathos, comedy, and tragedy. Unintended consequences seem to go in the opposite direction of our intentions. One could ponder how the stable leader of a school grounded in discipline and aspiring to self-knowledge could eventually end up as a train wreck. This is an appropriate and paradoxical question. I was confused and mystified by how this happened.

I spoke with Professor Fritz Koelln about this matter. He listened intently and said, "If such a gifted young person were to be born in the United States, there is no better person than John Gardner to work with him. John is so disciplined, so grounded and so American! John could help the young man more than anyone else." High praise from a demanding and discerning spirit! John was surprised when I told him Fritz's comments. John looked at me deeply and said, "Really?" John had inaccurately assumed that Fritz would have been critical and negative. John had not realized that he had a kindred soul in Fritz. I think the conversation may have given John pause and made him rethink his understanding of Fritz.

The whole experience tempered John, and he was a better, more kindly person after his departure. He learned from his mistakes. It was clearly a karmic moment for him and many at the school and shook the school to its foundations. You could be judgmental of John and the faculty. They were not able to handle a difficult moment. Easier said than done! Assigning blame is not curative.

John undertook a mea culpa. He knew he was the main player in this drama. His faults seemed ironic and almost tragic. This man of great learning, insight, and discipline was not equal to the task. This chastened him. John was humbled. Though he did not feel he had been wrong in his support of the opportunity this young clairvoyant had offered, he fully accepted his responsibility for the school's failure to make good on it. This is a heroic act—to accept responsibility even if it is not all your fault.

The school survived, but the loss of John and many of its fine teachers was palpable. The school seemed a shadow of its former self. The exodus of teachers gradually diminished, and the school righted itself, but a certain sense of esprit was missing.

Some of the teachers who left stayed close with John after he moved to western Massachusetts. There he continued his anthroposophic studies, entertained friends and rehabilitated a hill behind his house into a garden. He was an arduous worker. John continued to fell trees well into his eighties. Watching John use an ax was how I imagine Abe Lincoln might have. First and foremost, he had immense respect for both the tree and the axe. He would sharpen the ax. His aim was direct; his swing was forceful yet graceful. He let the ax do its job. The ax would crack the bark and drive deep into the wood. He knew how to make the last cut and fell the tree in the direction he wanted. John would split the tree into pieces appropriate for his wood-burning stove. John was known as Jack in his youth, part of which was spent as a lumberjack. Jack could walk on logs rolling down a stream and artfully untangle logjams. He was able to do this only because he had natural balance and poise. Kids, don't try this at home! In later life, he untangled intellectual logjams with grace and balance.

John could also convince people to work with him and help him clear brush, climb up trees to cut off limbs, and make order out of disorder. He firmly believed that work was ennobling and acted accordingly, even work that he found unpleasant. The important point is that the individual makes the work noble.

John led the school in numerous innovations. One such innovation was the work program, which had students and teachers working together cleaning the school at the end of each day (with students taking the lead in the high school), and at Glen Brook, the school's country campus in New Hampshire. John felt strongly that this was a distinctly American contribution to Waldorf education.

In 1971, Herr Tautz, a highly respected German Waldorf leader, visited the institute and classes throughout the lower school; he also observed this program in action in the high school at the end of his day there. Asked later in the faculty meeting to comment on all he'd seen during his visit, his very first comment was, "When I try to tell them back in Germany what I just saw in your high school this afternoon [at a time, young people around the world were in high protest] they would not believe me." John loved that! He rightly felt that such an innovation represented the essence of the true Waldorf impulse, and he had the leadership skills to get the whole faculty involved.

In Massachusetts, he held gatherings for friends and led study groups. There was always a hint of "Camelot lost," but John soldiered on. He started a study group that included a large number of people from Long Island, as well as new friends from Massachusetts. Since he thought that freedom was the goal for each individual, John was relentlessly an advocate for spiritual activity. Sometimes that meant that John would confront you if he thought you were slacking off.

I was fortunate to maintain a relationship with John and participate in a study group with him up to his death. He maintained his incredible capability to lead a group to new heights of spiritual activity and understanding of Steiner's works. John would create a vessel that allowed individuals to grow in their spirituality. He did so through his example of being open to spiritual ideas and wrestling with them, all in front of you. He understood that we are all pilgrims on this Earth and that, if we humbly ask for spiritual guidance, grace may flow to us.

John's thinking remained clear until his death. A good example (with his italics) comes from his introduction to *Education in Search of the Spirit.*

Thinking must in no way be considered "subjective." It is thinking alone that is capable of calling our attention in the first place to the distinction between subject and object. How can thinking belong only to the subject, when without thinking the subject could not *be cognized* as the subject, nor could the world *be cognized* as composed of objects? The distinction between subject and object is not only introduced by thinking; it is also overcome by thinking. Thinking takes place in and through the self, it is true; but its validity reaches beyond the self to the farthest world limits. When true thinking speaks inside the soul, it is the world itself that is speaking. The objects and events of the world utter their secrets in us; the thoughts we think—in so far as we let them develop life and charac-ter—are these secrets. But the secrets were already creative forces in the world before they became a comprehensible language in the soul.

If we hold this attitude toward the nature of thought, we shall begin to think quite differently from someone who uses thinking but does not trust it. Because we do trust, we will give ourselves to the work of objective thought with the greatest subjective enthusiasm and hope. We will pour our full energy into it and ask not only the mind but also the heart, breath, and limbs to join in the act of thinking. It will seem obvious to us that every soul power should be mobilized for cognition. In such thinking, our whole sub-jectivity is taken up into the act of thought—*and is thereby released from subjectivity.* The whole objective world, as it utters itself in this kind of thought, is released correspond-ingly from *objectivity.* When the soul of the knower has sacrificed subjective bias for the sake of pure knowledge of reality, that reality can in turn shed its mask of externality and reveal itself as living presence. When educators come to the right appreciation of the human capacity of intuitive thought, they will know how to build the bridge between self and world. They will see that the world can think itself in the human being. When it does so in the head alone, cer-tain truths come to light, but they are not the truth needed by the heart or bowels of compassion. There is no reason why the world, out of its deeper mysteries, cannot impart also to the heart what it craves, if only the heart will learn how to think. (pp. 26–27)

In later life, John wrote about his inner experiences. The themes are Michaelic and emphasize his openness to the spirit, silence, praising God, trust, and joy.

Sound the trumpet! The Battle begins.
Be ready. Be brave.
Look to me, for I am the warrior
in each and for all of you.
Let my victory pour through you into words and deeds.
Only so can the fight be fairly, truly, creatively won.

Hear me!
Open your ears to the silence in which I speak.
Would your heart know truth, quiet it, open it.
Quiet it in trust; open it in faith and hope.
There shall the sun of my love rise.
Let this sun stream forth to meet nature, to meet other men.
Return my love to me.

When you quiet down and humbly,
patiently, lovingly seek my guidance,
your old thoughts are somewhat canceled,
and new thoughts begin to flow.
Into the flowing of these thoughts my own word
    is somehow instilled.
They almost live.
But when you at last seek and find pure silence,
you will hear without doubt my living Word.

"In all things, praise God":
in sorrow as in joy, in loneliness as in companionship,
in defeat as in victory. Both belong to God;
He but uses the dark to strengthen your experience
    of the light.

Be glad!
The time of testing is here.
Hold firm, abide quietly in trust and good will;
see my victory unfold.
The old must be done away with, but
Behold, I will make all things new.

When his body could no longer house his spirit, he declined. The last time I saw John was in his nursing home; he was only a few days from excarnating. He moved in and out of clear consciousness. At one point he asked, "Who wants to speak with the dead?" I did not know if he was speaking to me or to someone on the other side. He repeated the question. After the third iteration of "Who wants to speak with the dead?" I assumed he was speaking to me. I answered, "I think we all do, John." He shot back, "No, Neill, you do; most people don't." Those were the last words we had together.

After John's funeral service Harry Blanchard, a former faculty chair of the Kimberton school in Pennsylvania, recalled his initial visit with John. He found himself suddenly very alert as he realized that he had never been listened to before with such complete attention.

I believe John continues to progress in the spiritual realm.

Johnny and Lee Lecraw

Lee Lecraw

"Trust in the ever-present help of the spiritual world."
RUDOLF STEINER

Lee (Adrian) Lecraw was born in Van Horne, Iowa, on December 13, 1914. Who could forget 12/13/14? She had one sister and four half-brothers. She left this Earth on September 15, 2012. At that time she was living in the Philippines with her son and his family.

I first met Lee when she was Co-director of the Waldorf Institute at Adelphi University. Lee was thin, with a slight frame that belied her incredible grit and strength. On first glance she appeared to be what was called "a lady" in the 1950s. She had a regal bearing. She wore elegant St. John's suits and pearls, drove a Mercedes Benz, and lived in a large home in Old Westbury, New York. There were cut flowers in her room. She had a soft child-like voice and was a wonderful singer.

One could assume she was to the manor born. In fact, her youth was the exact opposite. She was born on a farm in Iowa following her father's death when his horses bolted and he was dragged under the harrow. Her mother moved to California and married another farmer. Since she was born in 1914, she endured the Depression as a teenager and young woman. Farming is tough enough in the best of times, but during the Depression money was scarce and hard work was the only option. Lee's upbringing formed her character and tempered her entire life. Her high voice might have sounded superficial at first, but her depth was the result of a life that began in harsh circumstances. No one leads a superficial life; we all endure trials and tribulations.

Although Lee's early life was hardscrabble, she was well loved. At Christmas, Lee's stepfather carved a wooden doll for Lee and her sister to share. Lee's mother made clothes for it. Each Christmas thereafter Lee's stepfather would repaint the doll's face, which was worn away by the love and play of Lee and her sister. Lee always appreciated handmade crafts created with love.

When Lee first went to school, she had a very hard time understanding the language. She spoke German at home and did not understand English! Her parents had not prepared her for this educational experience. She quickly learned English and fell in love with learning. The ancient Greeks had a term for the love of learning: *Paideia*. It was not academic or confined to a classroom. For the ancient Greeks, *Paideia* espressed a lifelong love of learning. Ever determined and practical, Lee paid for her college education at the University of California at Berkeley by working in a sardine factory.

She went on to graduate school at George Washington University in Washington DC, where she met Johnny Lecraw, who introduced the farm girl to meals in restaurants and going to plays, concerts, and museums.

She and Johnny married and moved to Long Island. When she toured the Waldorf school in Garden City, the grounds and the art on display impressed Lee. She enrolled their two children there.

In spite of our materialistic age, Lee remained child-like, though certainly not childish. She was filled with a love of learning, beauty, and nature. She exulted in the growth of humans and plants. She was a gardener of the spirit. She tended her students, flowers, and gardens with incredible devotion. She was earnest in her nurturing. She loved growth in all its manifold manifestations, especially the growth of an individual.

She had an intimate appreciation for mathematics and forms. She made intricate string designs to illustrate the beauty of a curve in three dimensions. She saw the Fibonacci spiral in sunflowers and the spiral inherent in a nautilus shell. She loved the stark, crystalline beauty of geodes.

Her natural naiveté sometimes seemed almost comic. When her beloved Johnny took her to see the play *Wait until Dark*, Lee became completely engaged in the drama. At the climactic moment when the villain was about to plunge a knife into the back of the unsuspecting, blind heroine, Lee stood up and shouted, "Watch out, he's behind you with a knife!" Johnny gently pulled Lee back into her seat and softly whispered in her ear. "It's all right Lee; it's only a play."

Her ability to live in the moment was quintessential to Lee and to her connection with students. You have to be present with a child. The presence of a parent or teacher is formative to children. Rudolf Steiner suggested that parents and teachers should create the soul mood in which children grow. This is a mighty task and responsibility. Lee created a nurturing mood that allowed individuals to evolve.

John Gardner, the faculty chair for the Waldorf School of Garden City, observed Lee's nature and asked her to consider becoming a class teacher there. A class teacher is usually responsible for a class's first eight years of primary education. Waldorf school pedagogy follows the history of the development of consciousness. The class teacher has to embody the spirit of the particular age and teach from it. Each grade is taught emphasizing that particular perspective, such as the symmetry of ancient Greece in the fifth grade, the law of ancient Rome in the sixth, the creativity of the Renaissance in the seventh, and the modern world in the eighth. The teacher remains with the class for eight years, from first grade through the eighth grade. The teacher has to master a great deal of knowledge and make it comprehensible to each individual in her class, which is likely to include children with widely differing intellectual abilities. This daunting task demands learning and creating a new syllabus each year. Moreover, all such teaching is done from an artistic point of view. Teaching is an art. The teacher is an artist, as is each student. By promoting artistic activity from the very beginning, Waldorf pedagogy balances the overly intellectual, conceptual paradigm of modern education by nurturing capacities of feeling and will, as well as intellect. Intellectual activity begins in the later primary grades and becomes increasingly rigorous in high school.

When Lee was questioned by John Gardner regarding her extremely thorough preparation for her first class, he chided her for being overly prepared and sounding like a dictionary. She had left herself out—her passion, her ideas, her trust in her own intuitions. John asked Lee to go home and rethink her approach. The next day John continued the conversation. He asked her how she viewed her students. Lee replied that she tried to see the spiritual nature in each student. John put up his hands and said, "Stop! If you can do that, you will change the life of each student you teach." And Lee did just that, whether teaching primary-age children or graduate students. Lee stayed close to many of her students over decades and always held their best interests in her heart. She could see a person's strengths and weaknesses and help guide the individual to realize the individual's potential, from becoming a cook to running a major corporation.

After Lee had taken several classes through to the eighth grade, John Gardner asked her to help lead the Waldorf Institute Graduate

Program for Teacher Training. She agreed and asked John what her responsibilities would be. John just said, "Do whatever you think is best." Lee was flummoxed and went to see Sheldon Stoff, head of the Education Department at Adelphi University, who basically said the same thing. Lee went to work preparing graduate students to become Waldorf teachers. She did it by example, engaging students in actual classroom settings and elucidating Steiner's understanding of a child's spiritual nature.

Lee was a pioneer in her educational efforts at the Waldorf School of Garden City. It is not an exaggeration to say that John Gardner, Lee, and fellow founding teachers created a school that abides to this day. A colleague remembered Lee with high praise.

> Aside from being an inspired class teacher, she was one of the pioneers who—in collaboration with John Gardner—helped bring the Waldorf school into existence and increasing excellence over years. As one who felt blessed to find such a place to practice both Anthroposophy and pedagogy, I have undying gratitude for her and others who shared in the adventure. It was a deed of active faith, love for what does not yet exist, bringing it into existence.

Lee made you want to be a child in her class and to learn art, reading and math from her. She transformed twenty-three-year-old graduate students into primary school students. Lee understood that learning was more than rote repetition or intellectual concepts, especially for young students. She taught math by making it physically apparent. She had us walk in a circle around our desks in the room, reciting the two times table. Then at every number that ended in a zero, we walked backward until we hit another zero and went forward again. We made mistakes, laughed, and started all over again. The next time we clapped on every number divisible by four.

Lee enjoyed laughter, spontaneity, and absurdity. She once assigned us a show-and-tell exercise, asking us to act as third graders in our presentation. When it was my turn, I held my hand in a clenched fist and stretched my arm out from my body. She asked me, "What do you have in your hand?" I said, "a cat." She asked, "Why do you hold a cat that way? I said, "I'm holding it by its tail." She said, "That is not how you hold a cat. Why would you hold a cat by its tail?" I said, "It's dead." She broke out in laughter.

Lee was kind enough to join our Steiner student study group. Before one meeting she asked if an applicant for the Waldorf Institute could attend to see what the institute was like. We agreed. The young woman who came with Lee seemed odd. She did not dress in the Waldorf style. She wore a short, tight dress with fishnet stockings and combed her hair to cover her face. She also had an odd speech pattern and seemed out of it. After a while, it became clear that it was Joan Carr, the assistant to Lee. They both had a good laugh on us. At that same meeting we got into a discussion on infinity. I had brought a record by the Grateful Dead and asked Lee to listen to their song *Dark Star,* which reminded me of infinity. Good soul that Lee was, she listened to the whole song.

Even in her sixties, Lee was athletic. If a speaker did not show up for a class, she would ask us what we should do. With several good athletes in the class, we always chose volleyball. Lee would laugh, remove her shoes, and play volleyball with us in her St. John's suit.

One Waldorf Institute graduate student, who was teaching her first year at another Waldorf school, was having a hard time adjusting to the demands of being a class teacher. As they say in boxing terms, she was on the ropes and getting pummeled. Lee drove from Long Island and guided the young woman, who went on to become a stellar teacher and the head of a lower school.

Lee had a resolute will and would never surrender. She was determined to find the spiritual and to be active. Her spiritual activity ranged from teaching to reading Steiner's works and attending study groups to biodynamic gardening. Her will was evident even at the end of her life. She would sit with directed focus through six-hour study groups on *The Philosophy of Freedom* or at a Michaelmas festival. In all such endeavors, she put all her thinking, feeling, and will into the matter at hand. She eschewed nominalism and the merely abstract. Once, after hearing a prominent anthroposophic speaker, Lee's comment was, "Fine, now make it real."

"Make it real" was Lee's mantra. She had the ability to transform the ordinary into the extraordinary. She did it regularly. Every year she would invite people to her home around Christmastime. The first time you went you had no idea what was in store. Lee had created a full garden in her living room with sprouting roses, crystals, lit candles, a path through the garden, a stream, and a Christmas tree. When you first saw it, you became five years old. There was deep soil for the plants. I asked Lee how she did it. She calmly stated that there were five layers: 1) plastic drop cloth, 2) newspaper, 3) plywood, 4) newspaper, and 5) plastic drop cloth.

Then she moved yards of topsoil in a wheelbarrow to the top of her platform. She forced plants to bloom indoors and planted them at Christmastime. After everyone had a chance to walk around the garden, Lee asked everyone to sit as she recited Selma Lagerlöf's *Christmas Rose*. She did not memorize it, but acted it out and became each character, from Robber Mother to the cold-hearted lay brother. It was enchanting. A friend who'd been raised Jewish attended and said that she never realized what Christmas was until that special night.

In 1978, the Waldorf School of Garden City went through a wrenching experience and split down the middle over the presence of an institute student and Waldorf alumnus who had an exceptional spiritual gift. In the midst of this crisis, Lee was herself felled by a tree. She had cut down a tree that landed on another one. The second tree bent into a spring, and when Lee moved the first tree, the second one struck her. She was seriously weakened by that accident. Although in considerable pain, she nevertheless attended the faculty meeting and spoke directly on the issue. As usual, she clarified the dispute in no uncertain terms. Rudolf Steiner had said that we should be open to spiritual intuition. Lee tried to reach a reasonable understanding, but because of her accident she was too weak to stay and left soon after she spoke. The discord among the faculty remained unresolved, and many of her friends left the school.

Later, Lee decided to resign. As she walked toward the main office to do so, with a resignation letter in her pocket, she realized that if she left the Waldorf Institute, the students would be unable to graduate. She ripped up her resignation letter and resumed teaching for the remainder of the year. She became an outcast to friends on both sides, feeling like Poland caught between Germany and Russia. It was a painful time for Lee. Half of her friends had left the school, the other half remained. Both sides distrusted Lee and thought she was on the other side. Lee, however, was on the side of truth and acted according to her own compass.

Lee retired and moved from Long Island to New Hampshire, but she did not sit in a rocking chair. She and Johnny transformed a hill into a garden. She put in terraces, moved rocks, and composted well into her nineties. Most of the younger people could not keep up with her prodigious efforts and physical labor. The farm girl created mountainous compost heaps. Nothing was wasted. Even after Johnny passed away, she remained active in her garden. As she got older, she lost the ability to use her legs, but she could still weed and garden. Once she went down her hill too far and could not get back up. The only answer was to slide further down the hill on her backside to the road, where she was picked up in a truck.

During one winter in Florida, Lee climbed to the top of a thirty-foot ladder to cut down coconuts. She thought the coconuts might fall and hurt people below, so she took it upon herself to get a ladder and climb to the top of the tree. Lee was eighty-nine! A friend of the Lecraws had taken a picture and added a caption: "What is Johnny Lecraw's wife doing up there?"

As she aged, Lee wondered why she was living so long. She was not world weary, but she wanted to be with Johnny and other loved ones on the other side. She constantly asked, "Why am I living so long?" I found a statement by Rudolf Steiner that clarified her situation. He observed that Ahriman cannot stand old age, because it shows materialism to be a lie. Certain older people have worked on their spiritual nature, and as their bodies decline their work with the spiritual becomes more evident. Hence a spiritual older person can be the reproach to Ahriman's false materialism.

Lee and I had conference calls with Marjorie (Hiddy) Spock. Hiddy was one-hundred-and-two years old, and Lee was ninety-two. I was a mere fifty-seven. Lee and I read to the nearly blind Hiddy from her own translation of Dr. Steiner's *Michael Mystery*. Ever honest, Lee admitted that she did not understand a particular passage. Hiddy responded, "Lee, when you get older, you will understand." I could not resist the situation. I exclaimed, "Get older? She's ninety-two, how old do you have to be?" We had a good laugh.

Lee's students loved her and admired the art of her teaching. Kenneth Chenault, a former CEO and chairman of American Express, had been a student in her second Waldorf class for eight years. During the nationwide "Teachers Count" campaign, Ken cited Mrs. Lecraw as "his most influential teacher. I learned values that have guided me all my life."

In 2007, Lee was invited back to the Waldorf school and was awarded the Distinguished Faculty Award at the sixtieth anniversary gala dinner. That day, as she examined the school from her wheelchair tour, she kept stopping students and asking them questions such as, "Do you like your school? What do you like?" When the students smiled and responded positively about their relationship to the school, so did Lee. "See, they are doing something right. The students like their school!"

This may seem odd unless you know how Lee prepared for everything; she was consistent. Although Lee was in pain at the end of her life, she prepared her own memorial service and had us read and sing what she wanted for her service. We practiced Bach's hymn *Wachet auf, ruft uns die Stimme* (Awake, the voice is calling us) with her until we sung it the way Lee wanted it. We would sometimes start laughing—she was conducting her own funeral dirge.

Lee had us read numerous inspirational quotations at her memorial service. She had us read the following Rudolf Steiner quotation, which summarizes her profound understanding of eternal life.

The Moment of Death

As little as the human being living on this Earth can perceive his own birth when looking back to the moment of birth, as little as this experience ever stands before the ordinary forces of the soul—for through ordinary forces no human being can look back to one's physical birth (on the other side in the life between death and rebirth)—it is just as necessary that there is always the moment of death toward which one looks back. Death always stands there as the last significant event. Seen from the other side, from beyond death, this death appears completely different from what we see from the physical side. It is the most beautiful experience to be seen from the other side between death and rebirth. It appears as the glorious picture of the eternal victory of spirit over matter, and just because it appears as a picture, it is therefore the constant awakener of the highest forces in the human being when dwelling in the spiritual experience between death and rebirth. (Steiner, "The Mystery of Death")

Lee had the following lines from Rudolf Steiner on a cabinet in her kitchen in Marlborough, New Hampshire. She was earnest in her daily search for the spiritual. She asked us to read them at her memorial service. These verses are Lee's anthem.

FOR THE MICHAEL AGE

We must eradicate from the soul
all fear and terror of what
comes toward humanity
from the future
We must acquire serenity
in all feelings and sensations
about the future.
We must look forward
with absolute equanimity
to everything that may come.
And we must think only that
whatever comes is given to us
by a world-directive
full of wisdom.

It is part of what we
must learn in this age—

namely, to live out of pure
trust, without any security
in existence.
Trust in the ever-present
help of the spiritual world.

Truly, nothing else will do
if our courage is not to fail us.

And let us seek awakening
from within ourselves
every morning
and every evening.

The following quotation is Lee's last writing to us. Her words resonate with St. John's words. Lee emphasizes the same themes as St. John: "Love one another. As I have loved you, so you must love one another. By this everyone will know that you are my disciples, if you love one another" (John, 13:34–35).

Friends,   August 2012

I love you all so much. As I pass into the next world, my body grows weaker, my will grows weaker, and my mind falters. My love grows and overflows for you. Please read from the Bible about love and take it into your hearts. Love is the most important in all this world.

Love, with all my heart,
Lee

.

Marjorie Spock

Marjorie Spock

"The Michael Age has arrived.
Hearts are beginning to have thoughts.
Enthusiasm is no longer generated by
obscure mysticism, but by
inner clarity supported
by thoughts."

RUDOLF STEINER, *The Michael Mystery* (p. 4)

Marjorie was born September 8, 1904, in New Haven, Connecticut. She came from a prominent family. Her older brother was Benjamin Spock, the world-renowned pediatrician and author of *The Common Sense Book of Baby and Child Care.* She passed away on January 23, 2008, in East Sullivan, Maine. Marjorie was a dynamic personality. She was a Waldorf school teacher, eurythmist, biodynamic farmer, environmentalist, skilled translator, and writer. Her published works include *Teaching as a Lively Art* and *In Celebration of the Human Heart;* her noteworthy essay *Group Moral Artistry II: The Art of Goethean Conversation;* her gifted translations of Rudolf Steiner's lectures *Awakening to Community;* the majority of Dr. Rudolf Steiner's final work *Anthroposophical Leading Thoughts* (published as *The Michael Mystery*); and her translation of Otto Palmer's *Rudolf Steiner on His Book "The Philosophy of Freedom."* It is interesting to note that Marjorie did not write introductions to her translations of Steiner. She simply let Steiner's words speak to the reader.

Marjorie lived a full life of 103 years. In the hundredth year of her life, she produced, directed, and choreographed a video about eurythmy, followed by two short training films when she was 101 and 102 years of age.

Marjorie convinced her father to do something unusual for 1922 America: send his daughter to college. Before she enrolled at Smith College, she met a camp counselor who had taken art courses at the Goetheanum in Dornach, Switzerland. The painting instructor there had spoken of a wonderful dance program in "Door Knock" (as she understood the name). In an interview for SteinerBooks she stated that she understood these words to mean "Knock and it shall be opened unto you," and knew instantly that she needed to go there.

In 1922, at the age of eighteen, she left New Haven and went to Dornach, Switzerland, the headquarters for the Anthroposophical Society, founded by Dr. Rudolf Steiner. She learned German and studied with Dr. Rudolf Steiner. She learned eurythmy from Frau Dr. Marie Steiner, who would frown when seeing Marjorie walking around with a tennis racket. Frau Dr. Steiner asked Marjorie to stop playing tennis. Marjorie gave a simple answer, "I like tennis," and continued playing. She was present at the Christmas Conference of 1923 and many other pivotal anthroposophic occasions.

Lee Lecraw and Marjorie Spock were good friends and taught together at The Waldorf School of Garden City, Long Island. Lee wanted me to meet Marjorie, whom Lee called Hiddy. In the summer of 2006, I was going to Acadia National Park, and Lee suggested I call Marjorie about possibly visiting with her in East Sullivan. Lee was ninety-one at the time, and Marjorie was about to turn 102. Marjorie was one of the last persons still living who had studied personally with Rudolf Steiner.

I called Marjorie. There was a long silence after she answered the phone, then a deep voice said "Hello" very slowly and with two distinct syllables. I said, "Hello, Marjorie, this is Neill Reilly. I am a friend of Lee Lecraw."

Without missing a beat, Marjorie replied, "Then I guess we had better be friends!" We both laughed. With that, we started a fast friendship. She invited Linda and me to visit her home in East Sullivan, Maine (north of Acadia National Park), on a specific date and predetermined hour.

When we met, we exchanged pleasantries and started discussing Anthroposophy. Marjorie was no longer able to read and had a helper for reading and writing. Her mind, however, was dynamic and lively. She was clearly a free thinker and could discuss multiple subjects with depth and humor. She enjoyed a robust conversation and did not suffer fools. She was a true student of Rudolf Steiner.

At one point in our meeting I asked her what it was like to be in Dr. Steiner's presence. Her answer amazed me. I'd always assumed that Dr. Steiner had a dynamic presence, but Marjorie stated the opposite: "You would not notice him in a crowd." She paused for effect and added with emphasis, "...until he started to speak. When he spoke, especially in a lecture, you felt that he was speaking to you. Each individual in the room felt that Dr. Steiner was addressing a higher part of one's individual being and addressing questions one could not formulate but were deep in the soul." She said his voice was in some way his most astonishing quality. He spoke with authority.

Marjorie's conversation was proof positive of what she had learned from Steiner. She was an excellent listener. Each word you spoke mattered to her. She took in your ideas and gave them deep respect.

I called Lee and told her that Marjorie and I'd had a great visit. Lee was very happy. Because Lee lived in southwest New Hampshire and Marjorie in northeast Maine, they rarely saw each other. I told them of the wonders of conference calling where we could all be on the same phone call at the same time. They were stunned. We set up a study group. The three of us read Marjorie's translation of *The Michael Mystery,* which consists of Steiner's letters regarding Christ and the Archangel Michael. These are Steiner's last writings before he died. They are Emersonian in their concise nature. They are filled with powerful images that are Steiner's last efforts to help us understand the criticality of spiritual activity.

Because of Marjorie's failing eyesight, Lee and would I read the essays to Marjorie, who took in every word and made sure we pronounced *Mika-el* correctly! Like Steiner, she was emphatic that a spiritual being should be properly addressed. "How would you like it if someone constantly mispronounced your name?"

Marjorie explained why she translated those nearly final words of Dr. Steiner. In 1984 Marjorie had become concerned that she would soon die and that few would know of this treasure that Dr. Steiner had given at the end of his life.

In Dornach, the most cherished time was when Dr. Steiner gave a lecture. It was the highlight of the week. Imagine our collective chagrin when we entered the lecture hall, and there was a note explaining that Dr. Steiner would be unable to give the lecture. It was crushing. We knew his health was precarious, and this confirmed our fears. However, instead of the lecture, Dr. Steiner had written a letter to the members, which was placed beside the note. As we read the letter, we were amazed by its content. Here were direct perceptions of Michael, Christ, and mighty spiritual realities. They were very dramatic and extremely powerful. That is why, sixty years later, I felt compelled to make sure the translations into American English ring true to that experience.

Marjorie was adept and able to listen, understand, and discuss difficult concepts, even at the age of 102. At one point, while we were reading from *The Michael Mystery,* Lee did not understand a complex concept. "Hiddy, I just don't get it."

Marjorie replied, "Lee, when you get older, you will understand."

I could not resist saying, "Marjorie, Lee is ninety-two. How old do you have to be to understand?" We all laughed.

I would read my essays over the phone to Marjorie. She would listen intently and ask me to go back two paragraphs. She would clarify that Rudolf Steiner would never have stated that idea as I had written it. She would then correct the phrase on the spot, and we would move on. All of this over the phone at 102 years of age!

Our conversations were rooted in Dr. Steiner's essays. His essays are filled with spiritual percepts and concepts, and by reading and meditating on them we can bring them to life in our own souls. We resurrect them into their true, unifying being. Those images are filled with a Pentecostal fire. To understand them, we have to abide within them, and they within us. The following are a few of the quotations that inspired our conversations.

Quotations *from* The Michael Mystery

Prior to the ninth century after the Mystery of Golgotha, human beings had a different relationship to their thoughts than they had later on. They did not feel that the thoughts that lived within their souls were their own products, but regarded them as gifts given to them by the spiritual world.

Even such thoughts as they entertained about what they perceived with their senses seemed to them revelations of the divine, conveyed by objects in the sense world. Anyone able to perceive the spirit understands this feeling. (Steiner, *The Michael Mystery,* p. 1)

He [Michael] frees thoughts from their restriction to the head region and opens a way for them to the heart. He sets inner enthusiasm glowing, enabling human beings to give themselves in devotion of soul to everything that can be experienced in the light of thought. The Michael Age has arrived. Hearts are beginning to have thoughts. Enthusiasm is no longer generated by obscure mysticism, but by inner clarity supported by thoughts. To grasp this is to receive Michael into one's own being. Thoughts that aim at understanding matters of the spirit in our time must spring from hearts devoted to Michael as the fiery cosmic lord of thought. (ibid., pp. 3 and 4)

As the Age of Michael dawns, it may seem as though all of this were still remote from human experience. Spiritually, however, it is near and needs only to be "seen." It is immeasurably important that human ideas should not stop at merely "thought" but should continue on to become "seeing" in the thinking of them. (ibid., p. 7)

Those who adhere to Michael *radiate love* toward the world around them and are thereby enabled to develop the relationship to the inner world of their souls that guides them to a meeting with the Christ. (ibid., p. 48)

Michael's preparation for his mission at the end of the nineteenth century goes forward in a mood of cosmic tragedy. On the Earth beneath, deepest satisfaction is often felt over the outcome of human conceptions of nature, but in Michael's realm there is a tragic sense of the obstacles hindering the growth of a true picture of the human being.

In earlier periods, Michael's lofty, spiritualized gaze lived in radiating sunlight, in the gleam of the morning skies and in the sparkling stars. Now this love has taken as its dominant trait a sorrowing gaze bent on the human race. (ibid., p. 79)

A new macrocosm will develop from this "grain of dust" Earth as the old, extinct one falls into dissolution, just as the whole large plant grows up from a spatially insignificant seed after the old plant has fallen into decay. To see the Earth as everywhere a world in germination is to see it truly. (ibid., p. 119)

It is not proper for the spiritual life of the West to suppress the ego in pursuit of knowledge. The Western task is rather to educate the ego to perceive the spirit. (ibid., p. 139)

When an individual has matured to the point of sharing the experience of Michael's activity, there will be no impoverishment of soul in the experience of nature, but instead an enrichment. One's feeling life will not tend to withdraw from sensory experience, but rather to be joyously inclined to accept into one's being all the wonders of the sensory world. (ibid., p. 150)

Marjorie and Silent Spring

Marjorie was a woman of great conviction and had a Michaelic will. If she thought she was right, she would dig her heels in and not budge in the face of opposition. More often than not, she was justified. While living on Long Island, she became incensed that the state was spraying pesticides to control insects. She said, "No," and took the government to court. This was one of the first environmental cases argued in court. Marjorie kept asking the government for scientific proof of the efficacy of its policies and tried to get them to admit to the consequential damages to the environment. She was also incensed by the state trying to control the land. She felt a true stewardship to protect the Earth. The pesticides would interrupt nature's rhythms. Marjorie worked with Eherenfried Pfeiffer, a noted biodynamic expert on the issue.

> With her deep understanding of nature and as an avid biodynamic gardener, Marjorie's work took on an added dimension when, in the area where she and her friend Polly Richards lived, on Long Island, New York, the government began aerial spraying of DDT against the perceived gypsy moth epidemic. She and Polly, who helped finance the legal action, brought a case with ten other people against the United States government over the continued spraying of DDT. Marjorie and Polly were formidable leaders for this commitment to the health of the Earth; organic, biodynamic food was a life-saving matter for Polly, who was in ill health. For Marjorie, the concern was for her friend's health, and the constitutional right as a property owner to keep her land as she wanted it, free of government infringement.
>
> This team was brilliant, committed, and erudite. According to Marjorie, the "government ran roughshod over anyone who got in the way of the new technology. They brushed us off like so many flies." The federal judge, appointed by President Eisenhower, threw out seventy-two uncontested admissions for the plaintiffs and denied their petitions. From the summer of 1957 to 1960, when the case reached the Supreme Court, Marjorie wrote a report each evening after work to interested and influential friends about each day's progress in and out of court.

Rachel Carson heard of this and soon got these daily briefings because she realized that the testimony from the experts that Marjorie had found would be valuable for her own research. This case, along with a massive bird kill on Cape Cod, was the springboard for the writing of *Silent Spring*. The trial took only twenty-two days, and toward the end, Rachel Carson asked for the transcript. They became close collaborators and friends. Though the plaintiffs lost the case, they won the right to bring an injunction in court so that, prior to a destructive environmental event, a full and proper scientific review had to be made. Marjorie always described it, saying, "We lost the battle but won the war." This became the germinal legal action for the environmental movement in the United States. There has been continuous interest in this case since that time. (Rahima Baldwin Dancy, memorial essay)

Marjorie lost the legal battle but helped launch the environmental movement. She decided to relocate to a state so poor that it could not afford pesticides, hence her home in remote Maine. She wanted a safe environment for Polly, her animals, her plants, and herself.

Moral Intuition and Otto Palmer's book on Rudolf Steiner

The first half of Steiner's *Philosophy of Freedom* deals with epistemology, how we know what we know. The second half focuses on morality, putting sense-free thinking into action, how to translate ideas into ideals and realize them in life. Dr. Steiner used the term *moral intuition*. Ponder Marjorie's action regarding DDT. She intuited that the spraying of DDT would have numerous, untold negative consequences. She studied the issue extensively, marshaled her arguments, and did not let the extremely low probability of winning the case deter her from her self-appointed mission. This could be an example of what Dr. Steiner defines as "moral intuition."

Stop and consider what the consequences would have been if Marjorie had not taken such a principled stand. Would Rachel Carson have written *Silent Spring*? Would the environmental movement have been started at a later date? Steiner uses another term, *ethical individualism*. The individual intuits what is the correct moral position and acts accordingly. For Steiner each individual is a unique being, capable of free will. Morality is the expression of that free will acting in concert with the will of God. Perhaps it makes more sense for a modern person to substitute the word *love* for *will*, which can be misunderstood as egotism: "He has a strong will and uses it to bully others." When we use the word *love*, it has a creative connotation. To do the love of God is to act as a co-creator with God. Therein lies freedom, a freedom that inherently has responsibility for our actions.

> That is what constitutes what I describe in my *Philosophy of Freedom* as *ethical individualism*, which, though the book does not put it that way, actually builds on the foundation of the Christ impulse in human beings. It builds on the foundation of human attainment of freedom as one transforms ordinary thinking into what *The Philosophy of Freedom* calls *pure thinking*—thinking that lifts itself into the spiritual world and brings impulses to moral action to birth from union with it. It does this by spiritualizing the love impulse otherwise bound up with the human physical body. Because moral ideals are drawn from the spiritual world by moral fantasy, they lead to acts as vital as their origin, becoming the energy of spiritual love. (Palmer, *Rudolf Steiner on His Book "The Philosophy of Freedom,"* p. 27)

Marjorie dedicated herself to spiritual activity. During her last years, she focused on critical works by and about Dr. Steiner, who stated that *The Philosophy of Freedom* was his most important work. Marjorie was very familiar with this work and its critical-ity for modern times. One of Marjorie's important translations was Otto Palmer's *Rudolf Steiner on His Book "The Philosophy of Free-dom."* In it, Palmer uses quotations by Steiner about his *Philosophy of Freedom* and connects them in an overview of the importance that Steiner himself attributed to the book. The result is a stunning collection of quotations from nearly every year between 1905 and 1925 on that pivotal work. Each quotation shines with the love that Steiner had for his book. Steiner said that *The Philosophy of Free-dom* would be remembered a thousand years after he died.

Marjorie was dedicated to leading a free life. Freedom is the quintessential definition of being human. "Mortal man is en route to freedom. As mortal man goes on making the immortal man in him ever more conscious, he becomes aware of his freedom. *Man is born to freedom, but he must educate himself in order to realize it* (ibid., p. 55). Freedom is not license. It is developed by discipline and responsibility. It is powered by love of the deed for its own sake, not by anything extrinsic to it. This love motivates individu-als beyond their sense-bound nature. Love or spiritual activity is apprehended by sense-free thinking and results in intuitive think-ing that is inspired and reunites percepts and concepts in a spiri-tual communion that transforms spirit into matter and matter into spirit. This love is also known as agape, love of the spirit. It deter-mines the morality of each individual according to her understand-ing of the True, the Beautiful, and the Good.

Palmer's personal story borders on the incomprehensible. Dur-ing World War I when he was home on leave in Hamburg, Ger-many, in June or July 1918, Palmer was introduced to Dr. Steiner by his mother. Shortly thereafter he went to the Western Front, where he was taken prisoner by the French. One of the first letters he wrote while in prison was to Rudolf Steiner, requesting a copy of *The Philosophy of Freedom*. On New Year's Day 1919, he received a copy and read it for decades until his death. Imagine the irony of reading *The Philosophy of Freedom* as a prisoner of war during World War I!

Palmer realized that Steiner kept referring to *The Philosophy of Freedom* and started annotating where and when Steiner made a reference. Palmer's book is a compilation of these quotations. Marjorie wanted the world to know what Dr. Steiner thought of his major opus and translated Palmer's work into American English.

> I tried to show the nature of pure thinking. The thinking that can take place in us before we have related this particular aspect of thought to any external percept and thereby rendered reality complete. I pointed out that this pure thinking can be perceived as an inner content of the soul, but that its real nature can be known only when the soul reaches the stage of true intuition as it travels the path of higher knowledge. Then a person comes to understand his or her thinking. One lives into this thinking for the first time with the help of intuition, for intuition is simply living into the suprasensory with one's own being—immersion of the self in the suprasensory. (ibid., pp. 37–38)

Awaking to Community

Marjorie translated these insightful lectures that Dr. Steiner gave in Stuttgart, 1923. They start on a tragic note regarding the burning of the Goetheanum. Marjorie was present when the Goetheanum burnt down. This beautiful building was the artistic manifestation of the soul and center of Anthroposophy. Its fiery destruction was a sad foreboding of future difficulties. In spite of this tragedy Dr. Steiner marshalled his forces and continued. He was still giving lectures on spiritual realities.

Marjorie took the following quotation to heart. It sounds like a description of her. "If this anthroposophic life is to develop in a practical direction, everything it undertakes must be born of fearless knowledge and a really strong will" (Steiner, *Awakening to Community*, p. 67).

The ancient Greeks looked toward the end, the *Telos*. Marjorie learned to see everything as a seed. This is the heart of being creative in all walks of life.

> The Greeks saw the bird where we see the egg. They saw the finished stage of things; we, their beginnings. Those who feel their whole heart and soul thrill to the seed aspects— the seed possibilities in nature—are those who have the correct outlook on it. That is the other side of modern natural science. Those who start looking through microscopes and telescopes with a religious attitude will find seed stages everywhere. The exactness characteristic of the modern way of studying nature allows us to see it as everywhere creative, everywhere hastening toward the future. That creates the new religious idea.
>
> Of course, people cannot develop the religious ideal I am describing unless they have a feeling for the seed potentialities that each individual will live out in other, quite different earthly and cosmic lives to come. (ibid., p. 80)

For Marjorie, artistry and nature are of paramount importance. They are how we humans define our connection with the divine.

> We moderns must create works in which the form element speaks more eloquently than does nature itself, yet speaks in a manner so akin to it that every line and color becomes

nature's prayer to the divine. By coming to grips with nature, we develop forms in which nature itself worships divinity. We speak to nature in artistic terms.

In reality, every plant, every tree has the desire to look up in prayer to the divine. This can be seen in a plant's or a tree's physiognomy. But plants and trees do not dispose over a sufficient capacity to express this. It is there as a potential, however, and if we bring it out, if we embody in our architectural and sculptural media the inner life of trees and plants and clouds and stones as that life lives in the lines and colors, and then nature speaks to the gods through our works of art. We discover the Logos in the world of nature. A higher nature than that surrounding us reveals itself in art—a higher nature that, in its own entirely natural way, releases the Logos to stream upward to divine–spiritual worlds. (ibid., p. 81)

Goethean conversation

In *The Philosophy of Freedom* Steiner gives an overview of how we can listen and literally think what someone else is thinking. This type of listening demands the silencing of our own ego and giving our attention to the other as if her thoughts were our thoughts. Although the following quotation is long, it is crucial to understanding Marjorie's development of it.

Appendix

The preface to the 1918 edition of *The Philosophy of Freedom,* Rudolf Steiner says:

What is it, in the first instance, that I have before me when I confront another person? The most immediate thing is the bodily appearance of the other person as given to me in sense perception; then, perhaps, the auditory perception of what he is saying, and so on. I do not merely stare at all this, but it sets my thinking activity in motion. Through the thinking with which I confront the other person, the percept of him becomes, as it were, transparent to the mind. I am bound to admit that when I grasp the percept with my thinking, it is not at all the same thing as appeared to the outer senses. In what is a direct appearance to the senses, something else is indirectly revealed. The mere sense appearance extinguishes itself at the same time as it confronts me. But what it reveals through this extinguishing compels me as a thinking being to extinguish my own thinking as long as I am under its influence, and to put its thinking in the place of mine. I then grasp its thinking in my thinking as an experience like my own. I have really perceived another person's thinking. The immediate percept, extinguishing itself as sense appearance, is grasped by my thinking, and this is a process lying wholly within my consciousness and consisting in this, that the other person's thinking takes the place of mine. Through the self-extinction of the sense appearance, the separation between the two spheres of consciousness is actually overcome. This expresses itself in my consciousness through the fact that while experiencing the content of another person's consciousness I experience my own consciousness as little as I experience it in dreamless sleep. Just as in dreamless sleep my waking consciousness is eliminated, so in my perceiving of the content of another person's consciousness the content of my own is eliminated. The illusion that it is not so only comes about because in perceiving the other person, firstly, the extinction of the content of one's own consciousness gives place not to unconsciousness, as it does in sleep, but to the content of the other person's consciousness, and secondly, the alternations between extinguishing and lighting up again of my own self-consciousness follow too rapidly to be generally noticed. (pp. 224–26)

Marjorie expounded upon this capacity in her essay *Group Moral Artistry II: The Art of Goethean Conversation.* More important, she practiced what she preached—her conversations were open to the spirit; she listened.

> But true conversations have that power. As the participants strive to enter the world of living thought together, each attunes his intuitive perception to the theme. And he does so in the special atmosphere engendered by approaching the threshold of the spiritual world: a mood of supernaturally attentive listening, of the most receptive openness to the life of thought into which he and his companions are now entering. In such an attitude the consciousness of all who share it shapes itself into a single chalice to contain that life. And partaking of that divine nutriment they partake also of communion, of fellowship; they live the Grail experience of modern man. (*Group Moral Artistry II,* p. 3)

Marjorie speaks from experience and can state the truth in unvarnished terms. She continually pondered and meditated on Steiner's insights and then made them her own with her uniquely American phraseology and spirit. She did not live in the past and just regurgitate it. She lived in the ideas and realized them in her daily life.

> Indeed, the principle is common to all esoteric striving. Invite the spirit by becoming spiritually active, and then hold yourself open to its visitation. (ibid., p. 4)
>
> The hope of that Presence can be strengthened by learning to listen to one's fellowmen in exactly the way one would listen to the spiritual world: evocatively, with reverence,

refraining from any trace of reaction, making one's own soul a seedbed for others' germinal ideas. (ibid., p. 6)

Marjorie's essay could be considered a meditation upon the profound truth stated by Christ, "Where two or three are gathered in my name, I am there in the midst of them" (Matt. 18:20).

Teaching as a Lively Art *by Marjorie Spock*

Marjorie was a Waldorf teacher first and foremost. She loved to teach and never stopped. She was gifted with intelligence and verve and in this book, gladly shared her gifts with others. She took what Steiner had indicated in his pedagogy and made it her own. Her book on education is filled with practical experiences that speak with authority, from storytelling to arithmetic. Marjorie constantly emphasizes the student's need for an artistic pedagogy that nourishes the soul, develops the body, and quickens the intellect. She believed in the validity of Steiner's insights and put them into practice.

Steiner's pedagogy observed that each child's development mirrors the evolution of humanity. Steiner is an avid evolutionist. However he does not stop with the physical. He observes that evolution continues in the spiritual realm as well. Humanity's consciousness is constantly evolving both as a group and as individuals. Ancient Greeks thought differently than we do. Yes, there are similarities, but they had a different type of consciousness, though one is not better than the other. To assume that human beings thought the same way three thousand years ago is an act of revisionism and denies the greatness of both ancient Greece and our modern scientific era. The proof is right before our eyes. Five-year-old children grow physically and become a fifteen-year-olds. The body and consciousness change as we age. Teachers encourage this growth by maintaining harmony with those changes. Therefore, each student goes from a myth-like understanding as a first-grade student to a modern, scientific thinker in the eighth grade

Central to Steiner's pedagogy is the awesome responsibility of a teacher. This makes some teachers have the fear of God in regard to their task.

> Not only must the teacher love and reverence his pupils; he must make himself worthy of being reverenced and loved by them. On his ability to do so will depend his real success as an educator. It is not what he knows, but what he *is* that affects the child most deeply, for children instinctively seek in their teacher a model for their own development. (Spock, *Teaching as a Lively Art,* pp. 129–30)

To understand how dedicated and thorough Marjorie was, she listed seventy-nine books in the book's bibliography!

In Celebration of the Human Heart *by Marjorie Spock*

Marjorie defined her positions on matters of consequence in this book on the human heart. She is very definite on the importance of innocence, beauty, art, and imagination. Marjorie speaks in a declarative voice about love, but not in a superficial manner, rather with a rigorous understanding of this most human of all activities. In her preface she deliberately uses the word *magic* to differentiate from the mundane conception of the word *real.*

> There are two kinds of worlds. One, shot through and through with magic, is the real world, known only to very few. The other, mistakenly called real, is the ordinary world inhabited by the great mass of humankind.

Perhaps it is closer to the truth to say that there is only one world, which appears to be two worlds to two different kinds of seeing.

The real, or magic, world sustains, enlivens, and shines through the ordinary one, though most adult eyes are too dull to notice it. So people carry on the gray existence of prisoners in a narrow cell, wholly inconsistent with the greatness and dignity of human nature. But there are moments in even the most cramped and darkened life when the magic world makes its presence felt in a sunburst loosed from its realm to clothe ordinariness in glory, as when one perceives poignant beauty, has an exciting idea, experiences Nature's grandeur, is touched by love, or feels one's very marrow tickled by the feather of the wand of wit. Then life lifts to a human level.

It is a question whether, in the long run, the lot of man-the-prisoner is made happier or sadder by these all-too-brief chance escapes into a fullness that he senses to be the birthright he has somehow lost. But it need not be a matter of chance or considered an escape. The magic of reality is right at hand, ripe for the picking. This book is an attempt to depict the attainable state of soul to which the Tree of Life lets down its fruits. (Spock, *In Celebration of the Human Heart*, p. i)

As the title of her book suggests, the heart is the central human organ. By that she means more than the physical heart; she means the center of our thinking, feeling, and willing and, most important, loving. In other words, all that makes us both humans and individuals. "For it is the heart that never ages, though it goes on ripening into eternity. The heart is the eternal child in human nature" (ibid., p. 11).

Christ made a definitive statement regarding the virtues of childhood. "He called a little child to him and placed the child among them. And he said: 'Truly I tell you, unless you change and become like little children, you will never enter the kingdom of heaven. Therefore, whoever takes the lowly position of this child is the greatest in the kingdom of heaven'" (Matt. 18:2–4). This understanding of innocence as the key to divinity is later emphasized by poets such as William Blake in his poems *Innocence* and *Experience*. Wordsworth also captured this insight.

> Our birth is but a sleep and a forgetting:
> The Soul that rises with us, our life's Star,
> Hath had elsewhere its setting,
> And cometh from afar:
> Not in entire forgetfulness,
> And not in utter nakedness,
> But trailing clouds of glory do we come
> From God, who is our home:
> Heaven lies about us in our infancy!
> (Wordsworth, *Intimations of Immortality,* stanza 5)

This does not mean returning to an idyllic youth or lost Eden. That would be anachronistic. This is a remembrance of immortality that empowers forging ahead to the New Adam. This is becoming like little children, full of wonder and awe at the majesty of life. This heartfelt nature is the key to entering heaven.

> The doors of the treasure houses are kept locked for fear that irresponsible persons may go in and lay waste to what is treasured there. So it is also with the realm of life, which is the threshold of the magic world.
> The treasure-house of life is a walled garden, as was Eden. There, Nature harbors small children for their safekeeping. When they are old enough to *come to themselves,* she opens the garden gate and lets them out into a new world, a sobering adventure. When they have grown still older and mature,

some remember the garden and take the pains necessary to re-enter it. But this time it is not Nature who admits them, but their own re-enlivened beings, a higher nature wakened in them by their own efforts. (Spock, *In Celebration of the Human Heart*, p. 14)

Marjorie states that this combination of love, wonder, and awe leads to wisdom, which is intimately connected with art, the quintessential human characteristic of creating.

This kind of knowing with heart's blood and lifeblood coursing through it, is of the warm quality of wisdom.

It is, moreover, of the special quality of art. What is art if not a love affair between world and artist, artist and idea? It is a relationship whose every phase and moment lifts out of the casual, the everyday, the ordinary, into the arrestingly significant, the never-quite-to-be-repeated, the eternal—a state so blessed and heightened as to spill its living gold over even the humblest lovers, sages, artists, and the works to which it inspires them.

Lover, artist, wise man; is there an essential difference between them? They are three growth stages of the same perceptive and responsive spirit running its course from the more personal to the more universal—at the end of which the wise man is wise just because he has learned to do for every fact of his experience what beginning lovers do only in the one case: perceive the singular lovableness of the beloved object and envision its belonging in a larger picture. (ibid., p. 17)

Marjorie summarized this section with the following statement regarding a person who has freed his inner self. "This man is artist, lover, wise man. He is whole; he is free. He is perceiving life and magic. He is making them" (ibid., p. 18).

To free this inner self, imagination is the spark that lights the fire. Not an imagination tied to just the physical, but one that is connected with the reality of Nature.

> But no pupil of Nature makes any progress sitting by. This goddess is a magician whose sleight-of-hand pours forth creation's living flow, and the inner eye must be fleet to follow and the mind to grasp it. They are made so by building imagination into an active organ of perception.
>
> Imagination and reality have long been pictured feeling ill at ease in one another's company. The fact is that they are linked so intimately that there is no way to reach Nature where she really lives other than by the path of imagination. Since she lives as a creator in imagining, must she not be grasped by the sympathetic intuition of a like faculty? (ibid., p. 21)

Marjorie had an exact understanding of the spiritual nature of art.

> Those works of art endure that bear the unmistakable traces of their origin in cosmic truth, just as those springing from lesser sources quickly pass away. Creations out of the eternal spirit breathe a greatness that lifts observers into the realm from which they issued: they are revelations of a higher order. (ibid., p. 33)

Marjorie ends her work with a fitting statement regarding spiritual activity with another. "Can there possibly be any joint activity more profoundly satisfying than that of helping to free the unique human image in each fellow man? (ibid., p. 74)

Crossing Over

Marjorie maintained her consciousness until her death. She had requested to be buried in a red eurythmy gown that was sent by FedEx to East Sullivan for her burial. She requested a closed coffin, made especially for her by a friend. Her friends put one red rose on her heart and then eleven on top of her coffin. Her head was facing east. Marjorie had a fear of fire from candles. There were no candles. Her friends continuously read the St. John's Gospel for seventy-two hours after her death. "In the heroic development of freedom, man the New Adam becomes the Earth's deliverer from death" (ibid., p. 25)

William Ward

William Ward

*Out of the health of the human soul
and out of desperate circumstances,
the new Christ experience will evolve.*

*Trying outer circumstances
will become inner soul trials,
out of these soul trials
vision will be born.*

RUDOLF STEINER

William Ward was born in 1947. He was a native of Michigan and majored in English literature as an undergraduate at Columbia University. He studied elementary education at the Waldorf Institute of Adelphi University, where he received a master's degree. William was a Waldorf class teacher for twenty-eight years at the Hawthorne Valley School in Harlemville, New York, from 1976 until 2005. He had taken three full classes from first to eighth grade and was teaching the fourth grade with his fourth class when he retired to deal with the diagnosis of a brain tumor. He crossed the threshold October 5, 2008, at the age of sixty-one.

A theater lover, William wrote numerous class plays and festival presentations and collaborated in all-school musical productions. William was an accomplished Waldorf teacher who gladly shared his insights into Waldorf education. He wrote an afterword for

Waldorf Alphabet Book titled "Learning to Read and Write in the Waldorf Schools."

In teaching reading, indeed all subjects, Waldorf teachers are guided by an overarching principle—to integrate intellectual development with artistic creativity and practical skill. As a pedagogic method, this means that the royal road to awaken thinking and harness the will means engaging the feelings. This educational ideal of balance is supported by contemporary developmental psychology that maps the dynamic interconnections between cognitive development, emotional intelligence, and bodily, kinesthetic intelligence. Finding ways to balance and integrate thinking, feeling, and willing in education through daily practice has important implications for teaching reading in Waldorf schools.

Whatever scientific model is proposed as the physiological basis of thinking, it is crucial for parents and educators to realize that the spoken word, saturated with warm feeling and evocative picture content unlocks the treasure house of imagination and cultivates the ground of future intellectual development. The empathic inner world of imagination, resonant with associations and intuitions, expands soul experience beyond the material world into the world of meanings and ideas.

I first met William at Lee Lecraw's home in Marlborough, New Hampshire, in 2006. We were having an alumni meeting of Waldorf Institute graduates. At one point in our meeting, Lee asked William to tell his story. William later expanded on his story in his book, *Traveling Light*. He described how he and his wife Andy were driving during their summer vacation in Maine. He felt he had hit something. An owl had flown into the car and was killed. William was troubled by this sad accident and felt it was an omen, which unfortunately proved correct. Upon their return home, William became uncharacteristically grouchy. Andy noted his change of mood, which made William even more irritable. Andy then countered that this proved her observation, and that William should see the doctor. William finally relented and went to see their doctor. The doctor noted that something did not make sense and recommended seeing a specialist. William agreed and the specialist discovered a tumor. Immediate surgery would be required on November 17, 2005.

In December, following the surgery, the doctor confirmed that William had brain cancer, specifically Glioblastoma multiforme (GBM). The doctor said that eighty percent of cancer patients with William's type of brain cancer die within a year. The rest died in the second year—one hundred percent fatal is a sobering reality. In fact, William managed to live three years, which the doctors considered miraculous.

William Ward wrote a personal account of his encounter with brain cancer. By the skill of his craft, he turned the personal into the universal. Since William had spent nearly thirty years as a Waldorf teacher at the Hawthorne Valley School in Harlemville, New York, he approached cancer as a teacher would. As a teacher he was open to learning vital life lessons from cancer. William also battled cancer as a warrior would defend himself against an enemy trying to kill him. He fully understood that life, each second of it, is truly precious—not in a delicate manner, but precious as in the lifeblood that flows from our hearts to maintain life in all our cells. His many questions revolved around this perspective: How can I learn from this tragic situation?

What distinguished William were the gifts of his common-sense, spiritual approach, his childlike wonder, and his boundless good humor. William's description of an MRI process with the clanging and clicking noises is priceless.

I entered the million-dollar marvel of the magnetic resonance imaging (MRI) machine. Foam blocks were pushed against my ears (not tightly enough as it turned out). Head immobilizer down. Check. Periscope up. Check. I glided into my metallic coffin. Technician to sound booth, tin can intercom on. Check. Trusting William prays to the benevolent powers that he be found free and clear....

Blast off! A VERY LOUD SOUND instantaneously juiced my adrenals into overdrive: fight, flight, or freeze. Freeze seemed to be the best and only option.

KLANG...CLICK... CLICK... CLICK... CLICK...
KLANG...CLICK... CLICK... CLICK... CLICK...
KLANG...CLICK... CLICK... CLICK... CLICK....

Relax! Yeh, I'm OK with this. I'm not claustrophobic. Not me. I'm in the Lord's hands. God, that's loud! There are better ear plugs for a buck at the hardware store than these foam blocks.... I think the technician left too much air space.... Where is the volume control?... Relax.... Who thought up this gadget? (Ward, *Traveling Light*, pp. 9–10)

William covered a great deal of spiritual territory in his book, from Rudolf Steiner to Novalis. Tom, a friend of William, visited him. Tom has Parkinson's and was able to share what he had learned from his disease about the power of love and prayer. This reminded William of Novalis.

The heart is the key to life and the world. If our life is as precarious as it is, it is so only in order that we should love and need one another. Because of the fact that we are each of us insufficient, we become open to the intervention of another, and it is this intervention that is the goal. When we are ill, others must look after us, and only they can do so. From this point of view, Christ is indisputably the key to the world. (ibid., p. 17)

After his brain surgery, William recalled his experience during the operation as the Medicine Wheel that surrounds and supports all individuals with love and devotion. His description creates an image worthy of William Blake or Fra Angelico. William's turn at the center of the Medicine Wheel came during his brain surgery.

This is what I saw, heard and felt:

The eternal starry dome bathes us all with infinite light invisibly permeating infinite midnight. A holy, helpless child is encircled by a globe of spirits—hundreds of young and old human beings, wise spirits of the dead, and, behind them, angelic beings who know this infant. All the assembled host is spiritually present for his birth in the spiritual world (what we call death)—or will it be his rebirth in the physical world? The child feels blissful, surrounded by an ocean of love. He beams it back from his joyous little heart to the circumference. This intensifies the love streaming toward him. The shining faces of all these human and spiritual beings are visible one by one and as a throng. Each in his own way is eloquently expressive, filled with spiritual intention, generous, compassionate, receptive, benevolent. There is no sorrow or fear, only great good will and warmth. The Medicine Wheel of those karmically connected to the child revolves majestically, as beautiful in its geometric structure as a Mozart symphony or a multidimensional stained glass rose window. The harmony of the stars rings and sings in the crystal clear spheres of the midnight-blue Empyrean. (ibid., pp. 22–23)

William's rendering reminds one of the beautiful mosaic ceiling of the Galla Placidia, a nearly 1,600-year-old mausoleum in Ravenna, Italy (see next page).

William had stared death in the face and had been scared and reborn. William experienced spiritual fullness in his surgery.

In this epiphany, William encountered what he called "The Children of the Future." These children desperately want to be born and educated in Waldorf schools so that they can add their gifts and love to a very needful Earth. In a certain sense we are all Children of the Future—spiritual beings who incarnated on Earth to share love. That experience was the essence of William's journey of survival and his purpose for surviving death and being reborn in order to write this book. After his brain surgery he retained an indelible mark on his soul—he had been saved for a reason. William received the year of grace he was given to live and tell his story. All of his readers are the beneficiaries of that graceful year he had to write his story.

This experience is not just for William; it is for all of us and centers on how we view ourselves. Are we just materialistic beings or are human beings more then a conglomerate of cells, atoms, wishes, and needs? William experienced spiritual fullness in his surgery.

When we read about the way William related to his journey, we realize we are in the presence of a master storyteller. William puts the reader into *medias res,* the center of his consciousness. From this vantage point, we meet Andy, his lovely, dedicated wife, as well as his daughters and dozens of human angelic beings who bear his cross with him. William was not alone; in fact the cancer surrounded him with love! He was in a cocoon of faith healers who refused to let him go gently into the night. He went gently into the light instead.

William valued the incredible care and love he received from the nursing staff. As anyone who has gone through traumatic health issues knows, nurses are guardian angels.

> Prior to the respite of Ambien, I had several brief but intense meaningful exchanges with members of the nursing staff who came to check on me. Who are these angels of mercy who keep vigil through the night and bring encouragement and compassionate care by day? Not only was my cranium surgically opened, but my revivified heart could now see that these people were sisters and brothers of mercy. They treated every patient and concerned family member with respect, empathy, and understanding. (ibid., p. 37)

Finding meaning in meaninglessness and salvation in pain is the path of Christ. We have to go through the Crucifixion to get to the Resurrection. William encountered many wise guides on his journey. He quotes the doctor in a footnote: "At this moment, Dr. Leuenberger said, 'Cancer is a path to the Christ.' It was as if I had been waiting to hear these very words. My heart lifted, and I felt my hope renewed" (ibid., p. 180).

William understood the critical role of beauty in education and life. He waxes poetic in his song of beauty.

> I feel a didactic episode coming on. We may even cross over into the grandiloquent. Old habits die hard. Bear with me. Beauty is the breath of life. The inspired soul, intoxicated, opens like a flower to the sun, illuminating wide horizons of inner experience. Guided by the intuition, vision, and the unique genius of the artist, interweaving powers of colors, forms, harmonies, polarities, rhythms, light and shadow, imaginations, and beings lead the entranced observer to sublime realms of wonder, awe, and reverence. Beauty, nature, and her "worthiest imitator, art," lift the soul from the tomb

of habitually confined consciousness into day clear light. No wonder, then, that Beauty is the heart of education. In opening the heart, beauty lights the mind and fires the will. This is why all the arts are central to Waldorf education, to all education. The arts, the great educators of humanity, inform the soul life with heavenly human powers through music, poetry, drama, painting, dance, sculpture, architecture, and the "royal art" yet to be realized, the social art. Beauty sculpts the soul. (ibid., p. 190)

William in his recuperation had time to ponder nature and is surprised that nature, *Natura,* was always there, waiting for him to look and cast off the spell that makes Natura invisible. The spell is defined by Blake's "mind-forged manacles" that obscure our inner and outer vision to see only what is mundane. We are blinded by our own willful denial of the spirit. William turns his experience into a short dialogue, as if in a play.

Was Natura enjoying my enjoyment of her beauty? I should ask and listen.

"Exceptional dew you have today, dear Lady," I thought to myself. "It sparkles in the grass like little suns."

I've been waiting for you to wake. I knew you would love the scattered dew jewels. Do you see how legions of my spider fisherman cast their nets for the new day? They are catching nothing but pearls.

"How patient and alert they are... dear Lady, everywhere I look I see newness. Have you always been so radiant?"

Did you forget, my child?

"Help me remember now, dear Lady." (ibid., p. 201)

William concludes his reverie a page later:

Shhh. Friends, here he comes on his walk. Places every-body. Let's see what he sees today. Just try to act natural, be relaxed, at home in the world. Don't get your hopes up too high, but today might be the day we will be rediscovered…

Always I am rewarded with a small gift from a walk in the woods: the smallest treasures of mosses in miniature perfection, of sprouting buds and moldering humus, of an inconspicuous unnamed blossom, or scurrier on beetly business. Being fills every crevice. (ibid., p. 202)

The following verse by Rudolf Steiner became the North Star by which William steered his soul.

FOR THE MICHAEL AGE

Let us eradicate from the soul all fear and terror
　of what comes to meet us out of the future.
Let us acquire serenity in all feelings and sensations
　about the future.
Let us look forward with absolute equanimity to
　everything that may come
and let us think only that whatever comes is given to us
　by a world direction full of wisdom.
It is part of what we must learn in this age, namely,
　to live out of pure trust
without any security in existence,
　trusting in the ever-present help of the spiritual world.
Truly nothing else will do if our courage is not to fail.
　Let us discipline our will
and let us seek that awakening from within ourselves
　every morning and every evening. (ibid., p. 219)

William's puckish sense of humor leads him to a joyous ending, using an old prospector such as the actor Gabby Hayes talking like the narrator in an old Western movie.

> As we part, here at the edge of Death Valley, I feel like an old prospector handing over a weather-stained chart. "You take this map, sonny. Where I'm goin' I won't be needin' it no more. But while you're here on the earthly plane, I want you to know there is water, the *water of life,* deep down, right here. Yonder, atop Solomon's Knob, is the Mother Lode— pay dirt, pure gold, the Sun's tears. The way is steep. Just keep putting one foot in front of the other. Up on top you can see forever. Goodbye, God bless, and good luck!"
>
> Meanwhile, my lift-off has been postponed until further notice. It's a blessing, giving me more time to prepare for my journey to Holy Jerusalem. It's a long way, but I intend to travel light. (ibid., pp. 220–21)

This book has many levels and perspectives from the serious to the comic. At its heart it is a Michaelic book. How do I encounter the Christ through cancer? How do I learn from my mortal enemy? How do I transform evil into good? Cancer can be seen as another instance of materialism gone amuck—endless, meaningless growth. This is the modern encounter with Ahriman. Cancer could be seen as Ahrimanic materialism. Cancer can break the spirit. How William brings meaning to meaninglessness is beyond art. It is in the acquired balance of a spiritual life filled with reverence and joy. In William's words depicting his life, you can sense his deep connection with Steiner's path of reverence in *The Knowledge of the Higher Worlds and Its Attainment.* You can feel the importance of spiritual activity from *The Philosophy of Freedom.*

Traveling Light should be read by teachers, mothers, fathers, doctors, nurses, those who are ill and those who support the sick. In other words, everyone should take this journey with William. It is a cathartic experience that will transform the reader as he witnesses William's rebirth. By reading *Traveling Light* the reader will be filled with Love, Light, and Life!

William's Passing Away

A few months before William passed over, he started losing his power of speech. This incredible wordsmith was losing his ability to communicate. At Pentecost, May 3, 2008, we decided to have a Whitsun Festival entitled "William Ward's Whitsun, Whereupon We Wish William Well." William and Andy attended, and we read many quotations from *Traveling Light* to William. William glowed in the warmth of our affection for him and his book.

William's memorial service was on a beautiful day in Hawthorne Valley. Hundreds came to joyfully celebrate William's life. Many of his fellow teachers spoke of their great love and admiration of William; all noted their fear of having a classroom near William's classroom. William did not have a disciplinary bone in his body. His classes were artistic, chaotic, and very loud! They bordered on anarchy. His students spoke with loving remembrances of a teacher who believed in each person's unique gift and helped numerous individuals on their journeys.

William had pondered the wisdom of his parents naming him William. He broke his name down to Will-I-Am. He thought Steiner's emphasis on will had special meaning in his life. He resolved to avoid slacking off. Mission accomplished!

The Star of the Sea

William also wrote *The Star of the Sea*, a modern Grail story, to be published in 2019 by Waldorf Publishing. Andy Ward and many friends have made this happen. William has the final word.

A Final Word

William Ward created *The Star of the Sea* during his years as a Class teacher and as a teacher of the "free religion" lessons at Hawthorne Valley school. This story, told as a sequel over the course of the school year, was of great importance to William and to the students who heard it in his own words:

> The free religion lessons and children's service were inaugurated under Rudolf Steiner's guidance at the first Waldorf school.... In the fall of 1986, after years of study, a handful of teachers launched this work at Hawthorne Valley.... The lessons took place after school each week for the children whose families chose to send them. Every other Sunday, these same teachers conducted a morning Children's Service for a small portion of those children.
>
> Rudolf Steiner gave thematic indications for the free religion lessons, but relevant stories and imaginative pictures in English appropriate for the lessons are hard to come by. Of necessity, over the years, I have worked meditatively to create stories of substance appropriate to the fouth- to sixth-grade age group. As this creative process has evolved, themes have arisen in the stories that nurture the children's openness to the mysteries of existence, cultivate a living imagination for the healing work of Christ, awaken a spiritual connection with nature, dramatize moral challenges, and develop a feeling for karmic meetings. The year-long stories I have

told are not moralizing, didactic, or overtly "religious." They do, however, connect with universal spiritual themes: the encounter with evil, brotherhood/sisterhood, forgiveness, tolerance, redemption, and reverence. I experienced the unfolding of the stories and was inspired by the remarkable degree to which children remain open to such a journey.

As a Waldorf teacher with twenty-five years experience, I have been increasingly concerned that children with no religious life at home are becoming increasingly impoverished. Soul capacities for reverence and compassion are stunted among those submerged in contemporary materialistic culture with little vision for what it means to become more fully human.

Aware of the positive response of the children in the religion lesson to these stories, I dare hope that this creative effort may have broader value. I know that in childhood there is a hunger for true imagination, spiritual depth, and a longing for sources of wisdom. These longings are seduced and exploited by a media onslaught of decadent "magical" powers and grotesque, often demonic, imagery. What healing, homeopathic, artistic, and spiritual vision could take root among these thorns?

Note from Andy Ward

After experiencing such a positive response to these stories from the children, William decided to transform this particular story, *The Star of the Sea*, from the spoken to the written word in hopes of publishing it in book form. Sadly, he was unable to complete the book before his passing. He did leave behind extensive notes, hoping that it could be completed by someone else. After some length of time, I was ready to fulfill his heartfelt wishes. It was a great joy to again get to know Luke and all the other residents of the

Cornish coast and London who appear in his adventures. The story is exactly as William wrote it, up to the epilogue. This final section was created from his notes, with the dream and vision sections as he wrote them.

In His Words Again

This book is an offering, not a storyline to be marketed. Life will answer whether such a work may find a wider audience than the few children who shared with me the joy of its unfolding. Sensing the soul thirst of the young, I feel the inner necessity of committing *Star of the Sea* to paper. I trust that the healing waters of life and awakening that transform its central figure will mysteriously flow to those who seek it." (*The Star of the Sea*, pp. 102-03)

✝

*For where two or three are gathered together in my name,
there am I in the midst of them.*

Matthew 18:20

Bibliography

Blatchford, Claire. *Turning: Words Heard from Within*. Gr. Barrington, MA: Lindisfarne, 2001.

Gardner, John. *American Heralds of the Spirit: Emerson, Whitman, Melville*. Hudson, NY, Lindisfarne, 1992.

———. *Education in Search of the Spirit: Essays on American Education*. Hudson, NY: Anthroposophic Press, 1996.

———. *Youth Longs to Know: Explorations of the Spirit in Education*. Hudson, NY, Lindisfarne, 1996.

Palmer, Otto. *Rudolf Steiner on His Book "The Philosophy of Freedom"* (tr. M. Spock). Gr. Barrington, MA: SteinerBooks, 2015.

Plato. *The Phaedo*.

Reilly, Neill. *Songs and Dreams: By Seeking We Are Found*. Gr. Barrington, MA: SteinerBooks, 2017.

Spock, Marjorie. *Fairy Worlds and Workers: A Natural History of Fairyland* (2nd ed.). Gr. Barrington, MA: SteinerBooks, 2013.

———. *Group Moral Artistry II: The Art of Goethean Conversation*. New York: St. George, 1983.

———. *In Celebration of the Human Heart*. Gr. Barrington, MA: SteinerBooks, 1982.

———. *Teaching as a Lively Art*. Gr. Barrington, MA: SteinerBooks, 2015.

Steiner, Rudolf. *Awakening to Community*. Gr. Barrington, MA: SteinerBooks, 1975.

———. *The Challenge of the Times*. Spring Valley, NY: Anthroposophic Press, 1941.

———. *Christianity as Mystical Fact and the Mysteries of Antiquity*. Gr. Barrington, MA: SteinerBooks, 2006.

———. *From Symptom to Reality in Modern History*. London: Rudolf Steiner Press 1976.

——. *Goethe's Theory of Knowledge: An Outline of the Epistemology of His Worldview* (tr. P. Clemm). Gr. Barrington, MA: SteinerBooks, 2008.

——. *Ideas for a New Europe.* Forest Row, UK: Rudolf Steiner Press, 1992

——. *Knowledge of the Higher Worlds and Its Attainment* (tr. G. Metaxa, D. S. Osmond, C. Davy). Hudson, NY: Anthroposophic Press, 1947.

——. *The Michael Mystery* (tr. M. Spock). Gr. Barrington, MA: SteinerBooks, 1984, reprinted 2015.

——. "The Mystery of Death," from *Das Geheimnis des Todes. Wesen und Bedeutung Mitteleuropas und die europäischen Volksgeister* (The secret of death: The Nature and importance of Central Europe and the European folk spirits). Basel: Rudolf Steiner Verlag, 2005.

——. *Nature's Open Secret: Introductions to Goethe's Scientific Writings* (tr. J. Barnes). Gr. Barrington, MA: SteinerBooks, 2015.

——. *An Outline of Esoteric Science* (tr. C. E. Creeger). Hudson, NY: Anthroposophic Press, 1997.

——. *The Philosophy of Freedom: The Basis for a Modern World Conception* (tr. M. Wilson). Forest Row, UK: Rudolf Steiner Press, 2011.

——. *The Riddles of Philosophy: Presented in an Outline of Its History.* (tr. F. Koelln). Gr. Barrington, MA: SteinerBooks, 2009.

——. *The Science of Knowing: Outline of an Epistemology Implicit in the Goethean World View* (tr. W. Lindeman). Chestnut Ridge, NY: Mercury Press, 1988.

——. *Theosophy: An Introduction to the Spiritual Processes in Human Life and in the Cosmos* (tr. C. E. Creeger). Hudson, NY: Anthroposophic Press, 1994.

——. *Truth and Knowledge: Introduction to the Philosophy of Spiritual Activity* (tr. R. Stebbing). Spring Valley, NY: Anthroposophic Press, 1981.

Ward, William. *The Star of the Sea.* Hudson, NY: Waldorf Publishing, 2019.

——. *Traveling Light: Walking the Cancer Path.* Gr. Barrington, MA: SteinerBooks, 2008.

A Note from SteinerBooks

SteinerBooks is a 501 (c)(3) not-for-profit organization incorporated in New York State since 1928. Its mission is to promote the progress and welfare of humanity and to increase general awareness of Rudolf Steiner (1861–1925), the Austrian-born polymath writer, lecturer, spiritual scientist, philosopher, cosmologist, educator, psychologist, alchemist, ecologist, Christian mystic, and evolutionary theorist. He developed Anthroposophy ("human wisdom") as a path to unite the spiritual in the human being with the spiritual in the universe. To this end, SteinerBooks publishes and distributes books and utilizes other means such as electronic media, conferences, and other activities to make his works available and to explore themes arising from and related to Anthroposophy and the spiritual–scientific movement Rudolf Steiner founded.

- We commission translations of books by Rudolf Steiner not previously published in English, as well as new translations for updated editions.

- Our goal is to make works on Anthroposophy more widely available by publishing and distributing both introductory and advanced works on spiritual research.

- New books are published for both print and digital editions to reach the widest possible readership.

- Recent technology also makes it practical for us to reissue out-of-print works for the next generation in both print and electronic editions.

SteinerBooks/Anthroposophic Press depends on readers for financial support, which is greatly needed, appreciated, and tax-deductible. Consider a donation by check or other means to SteinerBooks, PO Box 58, Hudson, NY 12534. You can also contribute via PayPal at www.steinerbooks.org. For more information about supporting our work or to make a contribution, please send email to friends@steinerbooks.org.

www.ingramcontent.com/pod-product-compliance
Lightning Source LLC
Chambersburg PA
CBHW030844090426
42737CB00009B/1103